NEW THEOLOGY
FOR PLAIN CHRISTIANS

NEW THEOLOGY
FOR PLAIN
CHRISTIANS

John Baptist Walker, O.F.M.

'The secret of attempting to escape armed revolution is:
not to fear the term "revolution", and to understand it
in the sense of profound and rapid change.'

ARCHBISHOP HELDER CÂMARA

Dimension Books · Denville, New Jersey

First published in Great Britain in 1970
by Darton, Longman & Todd Limited
85 Gloucester Road, London S.W. 7
© *1970 John Baptist Walker*

ISBN 0 232 51107 1

All Biblical quotations are from *The Jerusalem Bible*
© 1966 by Darton, Longman & Todd Ltd and
Doubleday & Company Inc.

Nihil Obstat Fr. Michael Mitchell O.F.M.
Censor Deputatus
Imprimi Potest Fr. Urbanus Judge O.F.M.
Minister Provincialis

CONTENTS

To all who work
for the future

INTRODUCTION

TO SAY that Vatican II is over and done may sound suspiciously like stating the obvious. It is meant, however, to underline the very real danger that we should continue to quote the Council, five years after its closure, as though it were still the last word on matters of Catholic faith and practice. For this would be to forget the fact that the very theology that produced the council documents has now moved on to take up post-Vatican II positions.

It has moved from a broadly progressive stance in which the demand for renewal could be taken by the liberal as merely the call to reform and tidy-up a basically unchanging ecclesiastical organisation towards a much more radical position from which that demand is coming increasingly to be seen as a call to revolution. That is to say, theology is beginning to understand the gospel of Jesus Christ as a perpetual challenge both to the Church and to society at large to be ever on the watch and prepared to make those deep and far-reaching changes it displays as necessary *here and now* if the kingdom is to come.

The resulting attempts at outlining a theology of revolution are as distressing to the liberal progressive as they are infuriating to the so-called traditional and conservative Catholic. Meanwhile, the very concept of revolution is itself in process of having its sting drawn and being emptied of all radical content by being taken up by the ecclesiastically trendy and smart.

It seems to me that conciliar theology – if we may so term the outlook and principles that shaped the more important statements of Vatican II – moved off after the council in two main directions before meeting up again on the revolutionary issue.

Paradoxically, those ideas of Protestant theologians like Bonhoeffer and Tillich that were re-stated with such impact during the time of the Council by Dr John Robinson in *Honest to God* tended to draw Roman Catholic theologians in Europe away from the question of God as such and back to the question of the Church. For, as *Honest to God* had itself concluded, the deity is to be known most fully, not by means of philosophical speculation, but in the man Christ Jesus.

Yet this man is himself presented to us most completely in the understanding and belief of the Church. In other words, the only Jesus we can adequately get to know today is the Jesus whom the Christian community has, through the ages, been acknowledging, preaching and confessing as the Son and Word of the unseen Father. It is to this community that men must consequently turn if they are to come to the full awareness of the deity as a God who really matters to them.

The question 'Who (or what) is God?' thus turned into the question 'Who is Jesus?' Yet this in itself could not be answered satisfactorily without the further enquiry, 'What do we mean by the Church?'

Attempts at an answer, like Hans Küng's two books *Structures of the Church* and *The Church*, or *The Grave of God* by Adolfs, tended to look back at the Church's origins in the New Testament and compare what they saw there with the Church as it developed in history and as it appears today. Such works were truly *radical*, in that they went right back to the 'radices' or roots of the Church, and *revolutionary*, in that they demanded profound changes if the Church were to be true to those roots.

Criticisms of this kind made increasingly obvious the drawbacks involved in looking upon the Church as the most important community in this world of ours, with the human race a very poor second. Instead, if the Church genuinely exists to serve the wider community of man, then, however necessary Christians may hold that service to be, it will still be a work rendered by the lesser to the greater, by the servant to the master, and not the other way round.

So the feeling grew that Vatican II had been much too inward-looking, too 'churchy' and unduly preoccupied with itself. Were another council to be called now, it was widely said, it would be the human race and not the Church that would have pride of place on the agenda.

This intuition was reinforced by what was called 'the opening to the left'. By this was meant that growing sympathy for, understanding of and dialogue with communism that had first sprung up noticeably in the Church in France after the last war, had been introduced by Pope John into Vatican affairs and had come to be represented by a movement that, in Britain, the Slant group was to label as 'the new left Church'.

This new left movement prepared the way for a more widely-acceptable conception of revolution than the marxist brand that it advocated itself when it criticised the capitalist system as basically anti-Christian because based upon the exploitation rather than the well-being of one's neighbour.

To many, the condemnation seemed too sweeping and the solution too doctrinaire. Nevertheless, the work of the new left did draw attention to what Pope Paul was to call in 'Populorum Progressio' a 'woeful system' 'which considers profit as the key motive for economic progress, competition as the supreme law of economics, and private ownership of the means of production as an absolute right that has no limits and carries no corresponding social obligations. This unchecked liberalism,' he went on, 'leads to dictatorship rightly denounced by Pius XI as producing "the international imperialism of money".'

'This type of capitalism,' said the pope, 'has been the source of excessive suffering, injustices and fratricidal conflicts whose effects still persist'; and the new left were already spelling out these ill effects as, for instance, world poverty, the Vietnam war and modern racism.

Movements like the Slant group helped crystallise among Christians the spirit of protest that had already made itself known in Britain in the nuclear disarmament campaign and anti-Vietnam war demonstrations of the fifties. Laurence Bright, for instance, pointed out – very courageously, in the face of the swelling tide of euphoria that followed immediately upon the Council – that the liturgical and ecumenical movements, for instance, could mislead Christians into a betrayal of their mission. If the Church was meant to serve the world, and especially the world's poor, as Vatican II had claimed, then it dare not waste its time and resources on the luxury of pursuing its own internal problems if that meant ignoring or reducing to second rank the far greater problems of the world outside. Its primary task is to help create human brotherhood.

After all, problems about the visible structure of the Church – the role of the pope and his fellow bishops, for example, or the way the mass is celebrated – are really minor questions that hang only on the fringes of Christianity. Organisational elements such as hierarchy, doctrinal formulations or liturgy are peripheral to Christianity in the sense that they are meant to be but means to a vastly more important end, that of loving and serving almighty God by helping establish his kingdom, a kingdom that is nothing other than the fellowship of all mankind.

Much more central, therefore, to the Church's purpose is the work of those of its members who are actively engaged in the pursuit of this fellowship – in the Y.C.W., perhaps, or in the various cell and family-group movements that are springing up in our time. The organisational Church exists to foster this kind of activity; and if we find it is not doing so wholeheartedly, then we must change it.

On the other hand, the Church's 'opening to the left' was itself to be branded, in its dialogue with communism, as in danger of the same kind of self-indulgence. Whereas the liturgical and ecumenical movements could present us with the disedifying sight of rich, white western Christians talking to one another while the poor, non-white world starved, so now the Christian–communist encounter could well look like an affair of the rich white races that did nothing to help the plight of the under-developed nations who were suffering from the depredations of communist and capitalist countries alike.

The radical Christian today tends to be no more rigidly marxist than he is narrowly ecclesiastical. This is not to say, however, that he does not see, clearly and with great urgency, the need for revolutionary change – first of all, in the hearts of men (including primarily his own), and then in the set-up of human society and the running of the Church – if that brotherhood of all mankind for which Christ Jesus died is ever to become a reality. And the radical theologian, in his turn, is coming to look on his own task as that of explaining and evaluating in the light of the Christian message the revolution that is already on its way.

And it is here that the Catholic thinker in Europe has come to find that he is on the same ground as his counterpart in the United States.

THE TROUBLE WITH GOD

Catholics and the 'Death of God'

SOON AFTER Vatican II, American theologians began to feel that the discussion going on in Europe about the meaning and role of the Church had become altogether inward-looking and irrelevant. How could Catholics justify this self-preoccupation when all around them the 'death of God' theology was raging? Thus Daniel Callaghan, writing in 'Commonweal', was to criticise Küng's *The Church* as quite beside the point, as it contributed nothing to the far more fundamental debate about God.

The affirmation 'God is dead' is notoriously capable of so many interpretations as to be practically meaningless unless heavily qualified. For Catholic theologians like the Canadian Leslie Dewart in his book *The Future of Belief* it meant something like this.

When we Christians have hitherto talked about God, we have done so, very often, in terms and concepts borrowed from a more primitive past. We have based our pictures of God, for instance, upon the Hebrew view of him as found in the Old Testament; we have elaborated on and sought to understand these pictures largely through the aid of Greek philosophy; yet we have tended to adopt a servile attitude before God as if he were some all-powerful feudal overlord. To put it more pithily, we have acted as *Hebrews* when we tried to *imagine* God, *Greeks* when we *thought* about him, and *serfs* when we *worshipped* him.

The Primitive Picture of God

Our primitive ancestors thought of the universe as a simple, three-decker affair, made up of the sky or dome of heaven, the earth, and the underworld foundations upon which the earth rested. But they failed to feel altogether at ease in this universe. For the earth seemed a very fickle and changeable lump of matter, and the creatures on it doomed forever to grow up and come into being only to fade away, decay and disintegrate. The human race was in particular preyed upon and surrounded by menacing and mysterious forces, by flood and famine, pain and disease, all of which threatened it with death.

These forces were quite outside the control of men since beyond their understanding. They must therefore represent the work of hidden and superior beings – of gods or of devils.

Yet above was the changeless blue sky, all-embracing, boundless and pure. Accordingly, men began to think of the sky itself as a god, or as the domain of some all-powerful deity who, like the heavenly vault itself, was stable, secure, safe and all-embracing. And this father-in-the-sky must be superior, in consequence, to the frightening forces, the lesser gods and demons, that perpetually threatened men with extinction.

In order to exist more securely, to become more really alive, to escape the ills that surrounded them, men felt the need to placate this sky-god and win from him some of his own permanence and security and life-force. He might have rivals up in the sky, in that heavenly throne-room that (so near-eastern people like the Hebrews believed) reared itself up above the blue vault, and above the ocean of rain-water that lay beyond the vault. But if he would but deign to protect *this* tribe, *this* clan, *this* nation, on its wanderings or in its territories, then all would be well.

And so the tribal encampment or settlement would be centred round a particular sacred place or object that connected the people up with their god and brought him down to them. Whether it were a high-place or holy hill, pillar or tree, portable tentpole or chest, here, for this people, was the centre of the world, the place where the god was truly present among them in all his life and power and richness of being. Here he was to be cajoled and induced into giving peace and protection to the whole village settlement or wandering caravan. Here the sacred rites were performed by the priests, rites that kept the god's anger at bay, that he found himself unable to resist, that would automatically win from him life in abundance.

If a *neurosis* is the compulsion to perform some irrational act felt by someone faced with an impossible situation that he cannot otherwise overcome, then such a religion was neurotic. If we mean by *magic* some kind of activity that automatically forces superior powers to come to one's aid, then it was magical too.

The God of Judaism

One can see, in the Old Testament, how the Hebrews gradually grew away from the neurotic and the magical in their attitude to Yahweh, but how the process was not completed until the coming of Jesus Christ.

First, they began to realise that Yahweh could not really be portrayed at all, since, however close he might be to his people, he still remained a being apart. He was neither animal nor man, but a hidden and invisible deity. They had to try and cope, too, with the belief that he was present to them in the ark, the tent of meeting and the temple and yet at the same time had his dwelling-place in the skies and far beyond their reach. Then they were gradually to come round to the conviction that Yahweh was not just the best and most powerful of the gods, but the only God there was, and that his rule thus must extend far beyond the borders of Palestine to take in the whole earth. So we find them, ultimately, coming to see this God as a Father, not just to the Jews, but to all the nations under heaven, and one who surrounded all the peoples of the earth with his loving care.

Jesus came to wean those Jews who would listen to him still further away from the magical and the neurotic in their attitude to Yahweh. God was not simply an angry and fearful deity who

could only be placated through keeping certain taboos and performing certain sacred rites. He was a loving Father who was to
be obeyed and worshipped 'in spirit and in truth'. Again, he was
not to be particularly found within some special holy place. The
one true temple, the real meeting-place between God and men,
was Jesus Christ himself, so that all those who came to Jesus in
love and faith would find the Father in him. God was not to be
worshipped by a sacred caste on behalf of a people unable otherwise to atone for their sins and find favour in his sight, since Jesus
Christ was himself the only genuine high-priest of humanity,
through whom alone all men might find forgiveness from the
Father and offer him their worship. Finally, that worship, though
expressed in ritual form in the Christian sacraments, was to be no
mere magical performance to force the deity's hand, but was the
self-offering of his people's hearts and lives, their 'sacrifice of
praise and thanksgiving'.

Nevertheless, while purifying the Jewish conception of God,
Jesus re-affirmed all that was true and good in it. For he disclosed
to his followers a God who, as their loving Father, was indeed
more close to them and more concerned about them than they
could have ever dreamed. Yet he also showed them a God they
could not otherwise see, a God who was far, far beyond their
grasp, the all-holy and completely 'other'.

The Old Testament spatial imagery of a God who was always
present to his people, whether in the ark or the temple, through
his angels or on the wings of the wind, and yet was also unimag-
inably distant from them and dwelt in the heights of heaven, came
to be translated, in the early Christian centuries, into the Greek
concepts of 'immanence' and 'transcendence'.

The Scholastic View

Once the Hebrew pictures began to be turned into Greek ways
of thought, into ideas that were much more familiar and congenial
to a non-Jewish world, so Christian thinkers gradually evolved
out of classical philosophy what was to become the 'natural
theology' of the scholastics – that is, the study of God in so far

as he could be known and understood by the human mind alone, and without the aid of revelation.

Such a study brought one to the knowledge of God, not as Father or Lord, but as the 'Supreme Being'. To understand something of this being, one took the idea of the noblest creature one knew, man himself, with all his good qualities (the 'via affirmativa'), having first submitted the idea to a rigorous censorship, cutting out from it anything that could be construed as at all unworthy, imperfect or limiting (the 'via negativa'). The resulting concept one then blew up, as it were, like a balloon until it was of gigantic size – infinite, in fact (the 'via eminentiae'). And one called it God.

Supreme, immense, infinite, perfect, transcendent: however one argued to his existence, it was in these terms that one thought of the Hebrew God in so far as he was 'almighty' and 'on high'. His otherness became much more a matter of ontology than of cosmology: what kind of a being he was rather than where he might dwell.

Like the Hebrews and Greeks, the Christians too assumed (and in some ways still do assume) that the universe was static and triple-layered. However, the *meaning* of the different layers had become increasingly more important than their precise location. The heavens were not simply some realm beyond the skies, but stood for a whole way of existing that was proper to God and completely different from our own, since free from all the restrictions that are part and parcel of the nature of things here on earth. They were, in short, *supernatural*. To be on earth, on the other hand, meant primarily to be limited and hedged in by the laws of nature, by space and time, growth and decay; it meant living in the *natural* order.

And it meant something more. For man's life on earth was also marked by an inescapable subjection to evil. Human beings were open to temptation and sin, and to that growing isolation that sin brings in its train and that finds its full expression in the loneliness of the grave. Man's life in the natural order was also *fallen*.

But the natural and supernatural orders could and did interact.

Or, rather, the supernatural could intrude into the natural. For God, though transcendent, was also immanent; he did not remain locked away in the heavenly sphere, but broke through into this world of ours to be with his people, to free them from their limitations and to save them from their sins. And so Christian theology came to think of these invasions of the supernatural into our earthly lives as wonderful and freely undertaken, and yet at the same time as normal, necessary and definable.

First, of course, God has to infuse an immortal soul into a prepared piece of matter before it can be called a human being at all. Then, because man is sinful, God must keep on coming to his aid by giving him the grace of the Holy Spirit, helping him by his providence or even working miracles on his behalf. And so the supernatural power of God is forever swooping down into this world of ours.

Evolution and the Idea of God

By the time the theory of evolution had finally ousted the older notion of a static universe, Christians were already questioning this idea of the 'natural' man, who, having fallen from an elevated state of friendship with God, now required further supernatural help if he were to be saved. With de Lubac in the 1940s, Catholics too entered at last into the discussion.

De Lubac's position, which he held onto in the face of an opposition that amounted to persecution, was basically this. The bible knows nothing of the existence, either real or possible, of any purely natural man. All it speaks of is a race that, had it not fallen, would have enjoyed a state of blessedness very much like that towards which, because of Christ's redemption, it is heading even now. For man's condition was from the first meant to be one of blessedness and of a closeness with God that no purely 'natural' human being could attain. As soon as his condition developed sinfully, then the same blessedness was still held out to him, but this time as a gift won for him by Jesus' rising from the dead.

The idea of man being able to exist in a sinless state, yet without the help of God's grace, and the discussions about what kind of a man he would be, are both purely hypothetical questions. In fact, man has never known such a condition, and indeed he never will; he is always offered either grace or glory by the Spirit of God, never simply left to his own 'natural' resources.

The supernatural might be completely beyond the requirements of man in a state of pure nature; but such a being has never existed and never will. It is as normal for man *as he really is* to have access to the Spirit as it is for him to have the air to breathe. He cannot demand the supernatural as his *right*, certainly, but he can nevertheless rely on it utterly. He needs and is able to receive and come under the influence of the Spirit as part and parcel of his human condition and everyday existence on this earth.

This line of reasoning has since been pressed further, especially by the Dutch theologians Piet Schoonenberg (in, for instance, *God's World in the Making* and *Covenant and Creation*) and A. Hulshosch in *God's Creation*. Taking as their starting point the work of Teilhard de Chardin and the accusation that he failed, in his assessment of man's condition, to take into account the special interventions of God by which the human seed receives its soul and sinful man is saved and destined for the glory of the resurrection, they asked whether, in fact, this demand did not arise out of a static view of the universe?

If, by the processes of evolution, a creature has developed whose normal state is to be united to God and to its fellows by the love of the indwelling Spirit, then are we to claim that the powers of nature could never produce such a being?

If we regard evolution as the mechanical self-unfolding of future forms out of the seeds of the present, then it is true that non-animate matter could not produce life, or sub-human forms the human spirit. If we picture God as a non-evolutionary deity who created the universe in the beginning and then sent it spinning on its evolutionary way, himself meanwhile retiring into his changeless heaven, then we will demand that things of themselves only evolve into higher forms if they already and from the start possess within themselves all the hidden, dormant, embryonic powers to become such forms. On these premises, human life could not have evolved out of mortal, animal life. God must have intervened, instead, at the point where men were to develop out of their primate ancestors, and he must keep on intervening whenever the human seed is due to become itself a human being.

Coupled with this, the fact of sin and redemption will further require an intervention of God at the point where the sinner is to be justified. God must again come out of retirement, as it were, to give grace, send the Spirit, endow the human being with supernatural life.

The unsatisfactory picture of a God who creates an evolving world but then has to keep on interfering with it, putting his spoke in so as to help human beings, will disappear if we think of him as an *evolutionary* God. For he did not make the world in the beginning like a huge clock which he then wound up and left to tick on through time by the power of its own in-built resources. Instead, he is involved in evolution as much as in creation, since the whole evolutionary process is but the prolongation of his one creative act.

Our ancestors looked back to a time 'in the beginning' when God expressed himself by creating an unchanging universe. If we now accept the fact that this universe is in reality evolving, then this can only mean, in consequence, that God's *expression* of himself is undergoing evolutionary change. The transcendent and unchanging Father is immanent and present in his changing creation, shaping and moulding it until it shall finally proclaim his glory to the fullest extent of which it is capable. Then, as Paul tells us, 'God will be all in all'.

It would be wrong to conclude from this that God and the universe are one. Rather, the God who is so 'other' that we can say nothing meaningful about his otherness makes himself known to us in earthly realities we can in part appreciate – realities that are caught up in the process of evolution, and speak to us of a deity who is made known from within that process.

But it would also be wrong to imagine that evolution is sustained and directed by God from the outside, as though he were a celestial puppet-master holding all the strings. Yet this is precisely what we do if we rely upon special divine interventions as explanations of those facts of earth that human knowledge is at present unable to fathom.

Science has, for example, long since given us a perfectly convincing account of how thunderstorms work. We no longer have to regard them as displays of God's anger. By the same token, it seems highly probable that science will one day be perfectly able to explain how life on our planet originated and developed – including the human variety. There will be less and less room, in other words, to fall back on the notion of a wonder-working God who comes into his creation from outside every now and again to bring about phenomena we cannot satisfactorily account for in any more normal way. Indeed, a God of this kind, a 'God of the gaps' as *Honest to God* described him, is a deity doomed to become more and more irrelevant every day. He is being pushed further and further back to the fringes of the universe as science comes in to take over those areas that we once ascribed to him alone.

If, on the other hand, evolution is truly the prolongation of God's creative activity, then there is no reason to suppose that spirit could not have developed out of matter as part of the evolutionary process. In other words, the development of human out of animal life, the growth of the human seed into a human being and the fact that this human being will be given a genuine offer of grace, all these events can be looked upon as *natural* and *fully explicable in terms of evolution.*

They are natural in the sense of being normal to man in his present existential condition as both fallen and redeemed. And they are fully explicable in terms of evolution in the sense that evolution takes place *with* God and not behind his back or in his absence. For *with* him, matter can indeed produce spirit and animal life develop into human. Thus the universe is continually being created by him into something more and more real.

The more man comes to understand and master this universe, however, the less need he feels for addressing God in child-like or feudal terms. He no longer expects God to solve all his problems by direct intervention, or to manipulate the workings of the winds and weather in his particular favour if he prays for rain or for a fine day. He feels, instead, that he has, in this respect, come of age, and that he can best worship God by himself discovering how to cure human ills or ward off disasters. And he feels, in consequence, uncomfortable when called upon to pray in the language of the serf or of the infant.

Making God Relevant

If God is to become really relevant to modern man then he must be experienced and encountered within this evolving universe and as inescapably involved in human living. For, as Robinson and, later, Dewart were to point out, much of our trouble with God stemmed from the mistake of turning him into an object, just one more being (however exalted) among the many that we know, a deity we can hold out at arm's length and examine dispassionately, a God as much 'out there' as the old man in the sky of our childish fancies.

If God is to be experienced as involved necessarily in our everyday lives, and not as some far-off wonder-worker who every now and again interrupts the ordinary course of events by performing some staggering prodigy, then it will be as a God within, a God we encounter in the depths of our being.

Tillich and Robinson had already suggested that we do in fact make such an encounter with this immanent God whenever we encounter other human beings in a personal way. By opening ourselves out to others in love, we are in reality opening ourselves out to God and making contact with him.

If we are to become fully human, it will only be by entering into the human community, forging our own personal relationships within that community, offering ourselves to others. And if we fail to meet our fellow human-beings with openness and love, we feel deep down that our behaviour has been, not merely anti-social and remiss, but in fact less than human. We have failed to live up to that standard deep within us that urges us on to give ourselves to the service of our neighbour in his need.

This background deep within us against which our lives are judged and measured, this area of ultimate concern, is, according to Tillich, God manifesting himself to us as the very ground of our being and showing himself as necessarily involved in every genuine human encounter we make. The deity whom we thus find as immanent within and underlying the response we make to other people is a God we also experience as far transcending the limitations of that response.

Any transcendent deity, whether pictured in a crude and primitive way as a God in the skies, or thought of as an infinite and immense being outside us, or spoken of as a wonder-working overlord, is already dead in so far as he is a construction of our own human minds. Indeed, he never existed.

Instead of searching him out or seeking to define him and sum him up in a language only adequate for dealing with our own experience of earthly realities, we will in fact discover this transcendent deity as *a God who matters to us* if we look for him precisely *within* that experience. However we name him, this God of ours will be a God we find by entering into relationship with other people, a God who is inescapably woven right into the fabric of our everyday lives.

We will find him, indeed, in the heart of *The Secular City*, according to Harvey Cox in a book that was to have an enormous impact upon Christian thought in the mid-sixties.

Cox was concerned with taking Robinson further and explaining, in terms of that typical American construct, the modern city, how the death of God, or rather the rejection of a man-made image of God, spells the death, too, of the idea of the 'sacred'. If God is no longer to be thought of as inhabiting some special realm separate from our profane world, and if we are unable to speak of certain places or objects or ways of living on our earth as 'holy' in comparison with the secular lives and occupations of the majority of men, then God is to be met with right in this secular world or not at all.

Cox optimistically took the U.S. city as the symbol of man's progress and achievement, and therefore as the typical scenario or background for his meeting with God.

Within a short time, however, that symbol was to turn very sour. The fact that city-culture of this type is only open to the inhabitants of the rich, developed world, and that even there it is coming under attack as unsuitable for full human living, allied with explosions in the city ghettoes, draft-card burnings outside city halls, riots and muggings in the city streets, sit-ins and re-bellions in the city's schools and colleges, all these factors spoke instead of the need for a Christianity that does more than baptise and tidy-up the American way of life, but is prepared instead to condemn that way of life in so far as it is rooted in injustice.

The same experiences that showed up the insufficiency of Cox's white, liberal view of society helped point out, too, the inadequacy of the *Honest to God* approach.

First of all, in the face of today's overwhelming social prob-lems, a God who can only be described metaphorically as a field or an area inside us is as dead as the primitive God up in the sky. Or, rather, he is not worth the knowing.

Furthermore, this approach can be criticised inasmuch as it seems to treat of my neighbour as though he were especially provided as a means for my own further development as a human being, the agent who enables me to express myself more fully. This romantic attitude may be tempered by liberalism – though I profit by him in terms of self-realisation, I also do him some good as well, and enable him also to express his own indi-viduality more fully in his encountering me.

Nevertheless, the approach lacks that communal perspective that sees as my purpose in life the setting up of the Kingdom of God – that is, my self-dedication to the building-up of the brotherhood of all mankind and of a future community in which I myself and all my fellow human-beings will find our fullest freedom and self-expression in the giving of ourselves, without reserve, to the rest of that redeemed society.

The God Made Known in Jesus

This is the Kingdom that is preached and inaugurated by the Word made flesh. That it so say, although it is true that God makes himself known to us within the human community, that Word is vague and ambiguous. Though it is true that he speaks more clearly in the other great religions of the world, yet again we will find his voice somewhat muffled and inadequate once we have heard the Word of God as immanent in the man Christ Jesus and in the community of Christians, the Church.

In bearing witness to a God who has revealed himself to us supremely in this particular human being, the Church goes on to testify that we can only enter into relationship or communion with Jesus, and through him with the Father, by entering into communion with the people around us; we cannot love God without loving our neighbour. And though the doctrines and sacraments of the Church may, in their different ways, explain the Christian meaning of these human relationships, they will remain mere empty phrases or hollow rites as far as we are concerned unless making explicit a relationship with the human community that we are already experiencing and constructing in our own lives.

Or, to put it another way, the Church can give us the knowledge, through her preaching, that our entry into the human community is, whether the mass of mankind is aware of it or not, an entry into community with a God who is revealed to us as a Father by the Spirit or love of his Son Jesus Christ. She can offer to redeem and deepen our relationships still further in her liturgy. But she cannot substitute for our own actual efforts at loving God in loving men. And, without this experience of love, her preaching must remain a dead letter and her sacraments fail to make us Christ-like.

Under the pressure of events that only showed up more clearly the hollowness of liberal optimism, Christian thought in the United States gave up the luxury of trying to find out the right things to say about the deity and instead turned its attention to the Word made flesh, and to the Church of that Word, in order to see if the God revealed in Jesus had anything relevant to say to the present disturbed situation.

In *God Still Speaks* Gabriel Moran explained for the benefit of Catholics who wanted to remain loyal to their tradition that revelation should not be seen as something over and done, a sacred story from the past, but as something that is happening *here and now* within the human community and in those same turbulent events that are shaking up the American scene. For, if revelation is to be defined as God speaking and man responding, and since man hears the Word and responds to it primarily in responding to the call of his neighbour in need of his loving assistance, then revelation is clearly taking place whenever men try to put an end to the black ghettoes, the pockets of poverty, the Vietnam war. It is in events like these that the voice of the Father of Jesus is truly heard.

But revelation in that fundamental form remains vague and anonymous unless explained to us by the Christian community, the Church, with reference to the *written* Word of God, the bible. For here we have the closed, completed record of the way the Word made flesh, in rising from the dead, revealed to us the fatherly love of a God we were to worship, not by retiring from the world, but by entering into it to protest against sin and division by trying to create community and brotherhood among men. The scriptures, then, provide the historical norm by which our present-day encounters with our fellows can be seen for what they are meant to be – encounters with the Christ who, in his Spirit, speaks to us through the lives of the poor and reveals to us the Father.

This means that the Catholic Church, if it is really to preach the Gospel of Christ according to the spirit of the times, must itself have something to say – and not as a mere aside but as an integral part of its message – about the evident evils in American society and in the world at large – about the denial of equal rights to the black population; about the rampant exploitation of the poor by the profiteers; and about the repression and bloodshed to which such activities inescapably lead.

As an institution and in its official statements of policy, the U.S. Church seemed to some of its members to be tolerating, if not actually siding with, white domination, unbridled capitalism and the unimaginable horror of the Vietnam war. The reactions have been both widespread and violent. Layfolk have taken to picketing bishops' offices or occupying church buildings to protest against the apparent lack of concern shown by the ecclesiastical authorities towards such problems. Priests are leaving their ministries and nuns their convents at an unprecedented rate to search for what they hope will be better ways of living the gospel in today's world than they feel the Church structures at present allow. Grievances have been aired and demands for change made in books like Kavanaugh's *A Modern Priest Looks At His Outdated Church*, or Moran's *Vision and Tactics: Towards an Adult Church*, or in widely selling periodicals like *Commonweal*, *The Critic* or the now somewhat notorious *National Catholic Reporter*.

But perhaps the most impressive and disturbing protest has come with the growth of the so-called 'underground Church', in which assemblies of Christians, dissatisfied with what they consider to be the unjustifiable foot-dragging of institutional religion, try and discover ways of witness and worship that they feel will make better sense in the present American scene. Their demand is for the Church to change radically in order to be in a position to say something relevant to the present revolutionary mood of great sections of the population both of the United States and of the world.

Indeed, the violence with which this demand is made often seems to us, in our staid and overcrowded little island, as alarmingly aggressive and at times distressingly immature. We can hardly find encouragement, for instance, in the report that a number of ex-priests claim to find their present managerial posts in, of all places, Wall Street, as 'more meaningful' ways of Christian living than their former occupations!

None the less, the enormous vitality of the American move-

ment towards a Christian understanding of revolutionary change
has brought Catholic theologians in the States not only to meeting
with their European colleagues on the same ground, but to their
contributing some of that vitality and freshness to the discussion.
Together they are now embarked on a common enquiry, not into
the death of God, but into the person of Jesus the Word and into
the nature and task of his Church.

2

THE VOCATION OF JESUS

Who is Jesus?

THE DISCUSSION about God has now centred itself largely upon the question of Jesus and of the Christian Church, an institution that, as it looks back to the written records it accepted in its beginnings as an adequate account of what it believed about Jesus, goes on today to witness to the belief that this particular human being reveals to us all we need to know and the most we can fruitfully say about the deity.

The man Jesus, according to Christianity, is the living image of what God is really like towards men. In other words, Jesus reduces the deity to human terms. And this will not scandalise or distress us if we remember that it also emphasises the fact that God is so far beyond the grasp of our minds or imaginations that he would remain utterly incomprehensible to us unless he made himself known to us in ways that we could understand. He speaks his revealing Word, therefore, from out of this world of men, so that we may hear it when we contemplate the natural universe, when we enter into communication with our fellow human beings, through our membership of one or other of the world's religions, and, supremely and most fully, in the life of Jesus of Nazareth.

'Philip said, "Lord, let us see the Father and then we shall be satisfied." "Have I been with you all this time, Philip," said Jesus to him, "and you still do not know me? To have seen me is to have seen the Father"' (John 14:8, 9).

Who exactly *is* this Jesus who 'lets us see the Father'? According to the bible, he is both *Word* of God and *Son* of God. But this simple statement has undergone such different interpretations and received so many shades of emphasis throughout the centuries that it would perhaps be as well to outline these changing viewpoints very briefly before looking at the question as it is being raised today.

In the early years of Christianity, interest tended to focus itself upon the question of Jesus' human-ness. Was he really and completely a man like us, a genuine human being who shared our fallen condition during his life on earth, or was his humanity merely some kind of disguise, a phantom cloak in which his divinity shrouded itself? By the fourth century, the belief in the true and full humanity of Jesus had become so firmly established that vast numbers of Christians doubted whether he was, in fact, anything *more* than a man, albeit an exceptionally good one. In particular, the rise of Arianism, with its open denial of the divinity of Christ, led to an over-reaction on the Catholic side that has been present in mainstream Christianity ever since in the form of an exaggerated emphasis on Jesus' godhead to the near exclusion of his manhood.

The scholastics of medieval Europe gave further theological backing to this tendency when they spoke of the earthly Jesus as a 'perfect man'. Because of their inadequate theory of how we had been saved, an explanation that simply required a God-man to pay back to the Father, on behalf of the rest of men, the infinite debt their sins had incurred, it seemed quite unnecessary and therefore most unfitting that Jesus should ever have shared our fallen state or allowed himself to feel any of its ill effects. Such drawbacks to ordinary human living as worry or weariness, disease or ignorance, pain or temptation could not have been an *inevitable* part of his normal experience. The crucifixion, they felt, could only have come about because, as a man, he freely *allowed* himself to suffer and to die, by way of exception, as it were.

The start of the present century, however, saw the development of a different and more scriptural explanation of the way we were redeemed, based upon Paul's clear teaching that, though Jesus' 'state was divine, yet he did not cling to his equality with God, but *emptied himself* to assume the condition of a slave, and became as men are; and being as all men are, he was humbler yet, even to accepting death, death on a cross. But God raised him high', to be 'Christ' and 'Lord' (Phil. 2:6–11).

This theology of the self-emptying or 'kenosis' of Jesus grew in turn into the richer theology of the 'paschal mystery' that was so strongly endorsed by Vatican II. This tried to show how we are only saved from our sins because the Son of God became truly a member of our fallen race, 'like us in every way, sin excepted', and open, in consequence, to the limitations of our earthly existence, to the onslaught of evil and the tyranny of death. For it was by his rising from the grave to a life of everlasting glory, free forever from the grip of evil, that he was able to change our fallen human condition and make of it the means by which we, too, could share in this new life of his.

We are not concerned here, however, with this theology of kenosis and the paschal mystery in so far as it explains the process of redemption, for this is a subject that has already been very widely tackled.[1] Our problem today is much more fundamental. For any meaning or value we might attach to the things Jesus did in order to save us will depend entirely upon whom we believe him to be.

This question, raised nearly three-quarters of a century ago by other Christians as a natural outcome of their discussions on kenosis but silenced among Roman Catholics in the general suppression of Modernism, has only recently been heard once more among us.

The Knowledge of Jesus

And it began with questions about Jesus' knowledge. If he was really a human being, with an understanding like our own, how did he get to know things? Did he have to learn, as we do, what his life was all about, or was special information fed into his mind by God from the very start? In particular, was he always aware

[1] See, for example, *For All Men*, John Baptist Walker, Darton, Longman & Todd. 1968.

of his own unique position as Son of God and of his future destiny through death to resurrection?

The medieval schoolmen, of course, solved this question quite simply. As a perfect man, Jesus had a perfect human intelligence. Thus, though he did, on one level, or with one part of his mind, have to learn how to walk and to speak and to develop as a human being, yet on another level he knew absolutely everything it was possible for a man to know, since this knowledge was poured into him by his Father from the first moment of his existence; hence the passages in the meditation books that would have us contemplate the frustration felt by Jesus when, fully conscious and knowing all things, he had to submit to the solitary confinement of nine months' imprisonment in his mother's womb. However, he generally refused to take advantage of this 'infused knowledge' in his day-to-day living, simply relying upon it to furnish him with the details of his mission. Over and above that, it was claimed – though not without some difficulty – that he 'beheld the face of God continually', just as the blessed do in heaven, and was thus, like them, always perfectly happy and contented, except when he deliberately switched off this 'beatific vision' in order to suffer the pains of his passion.

If, instead of asking what kind of a man the Son of God *could* have become in theory, we ask instead what kind of a man *did* he become in fact, then we will rightly refuse to credit him with superhuman ways of knowing things and stress that Jesus had genuinely to discover, just as we do, how to live as a human being. The synoptic gospels themselves clearly imply that he only gradually came to understand about his mission and about the suffering it would bring, so that it was not until after his baptism, as he saw the opposition to his message mounting, that they have him speaking of execution as the certain outcome of his preaching, and referring to it, furthermore, as another baptism.

Though there is general agreement among Roman Catholic theologians that Jesus must always have been in some way aware of his special relationship with God as Son to Father and of his special relationship with mankind as Word from God, this awareness does not necessarily mean that he knew consciously who he was and what he was meant to do, but rather that to be Son and Word was so constitutive of his very being that it coloured the whole of his life. Only as his consciousness dawned and developed would the conviction that he was God's Son and Word have grown correspondingly more articulate and clear.

But was this knowledge itself so prodigious and strange a thing as to tell against the idea that he really emptied himself of the glory that was his due, or did Jesus become so fully one of us that his growing consciousness of his being, in a very special way, Son of God and Son of Man, can be seen simply as that developing self-awareness that all human beings normally experience?

Our present understanding of the paschal mystery makes us prefer to think that, like us, Jesus learned more explicitly the kind of man he was and the kind of life he should lead the more he grew to maturity and entered into adult relationships with other people. But how does such a view square with the doctrine that Jesus is divine as well as human, and that it is here that his uniqueness resides?

The Uniqueness of Jesus

Before we can discuss this question with profit, we must first try to discover what it is that makes *any* human being different and distinct from any other. What is it, in fact, that stamps each one of us out as an individual and differentiates us from our fellows? Not merely the fact that each of us has a separate bodily existence, surely. Not just the differences in our fingerprints or passport photographs.

Star differs from star, stone from stone. What we are looking for, however, is something that singles us out on the *human* level.

And that 'something' would seem to be found in the fact that each one of us is related to other people – to our families, to the wider communities in which we live and ultimately to the race as a whole – in a particular, inimitable, unrepeatable way that is ours and ours alone. No one else can stand in precisely our position on the human landscape or share precisely our way of being linked up into the human family.

For this special relationship each one of us has with mankind as a whole is itself the product of a long chain, a wide-flung web of relationships that stretches right back to the beginnings of the race and right out to cover all its ramifications. These interwoven relationships produced, in fact, our own family circle and the man and woman out of whose own special relationship we were ultimately born. In other words, we enter the race with ready-made relatives, with parentage and a family tree that connects us up to the entire human community. Thus we stand in our own special place in the world because of the unique way each one of us is related, first towards the other members of our immediate family circle, and, through them, towards the human race as a whole.

And all those relationships out of which we were born have bequeathed to us our own individual make-up. We have inherited from the gene-bank of the human community those characteristics that were selected out for us by the particular time and manner in which we entered the race and were inserted into the network of relationships that binds it together.

As we shall see, our approach towards God is experienced by approaching our fellow men. It follows, therefore, that our individual relationships with God will be unique precisely because of the uniqueness of our relationships with mankind. Since each one of us is able to enter into communication with other people in a way that is inimitably ours alone, this will be the particular way in which we shall also communicate, whether knowingly or not, with the deity.

Relation produces *vocation*. In other words, the way we exist from the outset as individuals, each with our own particular set of relationships with the rest of the race and that unrepeatable blend of personal characteristics that we have inherited, through those relationships, *from* the race, will largely determine what we may or will become in life by opening out to us a certain specific range of options and possibilities.

Of themselves, these given relationships will remain inert and inactive. It is up to us to live them out and to humanise them by deepening and expanding them (with the help of our inborn characteristics) into real fellowship, or love. In doing so, we will also be activating and deepening our special relationship with God, entering further into loving fellowship with him in that unique way that has been ours alone from the moment we began to exist. Thus each of us has his own personal vocation – to live out, in a uniquely characteristic way, the equally unique relationship with God and men into which he was born.

We may say the same about Jesus. As a man, he too was differentiated from all other human beings by the particular relationship towards God and men which was his from the start of his human existence, in that he was distinctively Son towards God and Word towards mankind. And these are not separate relationships, but just two facets of the *same* relationship because, to be truly the *Word* of God – not just a messenger from him, that is, but a real *communication* or self-giving of the deity to man – Jesus must also be truly the *Son* of God and somehow *identifiable* with him.

Jesus had the individual vocation, therefore, of activating, living out and developing this two-fold relationship to its fullest human dimensions. This he could only do, however, by means of those characteristics and that special position in the human race that had been handed down to him from the race itself and particularly from his own people and their history.

Before he could give himself fully as Son to the Father and as Word to humanity, he had difficulties to surmount, obstacles to overcome. And the continual struggle that ensued dedicated Jesus both to death and to new life.

As a mortal human being, he experienced all those features of life on this earth that tend to drag a man down and draw him away from his fellows and his God. He felt those limitations to human freedom, to full development and to perfect unity with the heavenly Father and with men that characterise our fallen human state. And he conquered them.

Jesus strove as Word to give the Father's message to men.

But his efforts were drastically confined. First, sin hardened men's hearts against this message. Second, the effectiveness of his preaching was limited by the laws of space, time and mortality. Jesus could only be at one place at one particular time. He could only address himself to the small group of people who happened to be at hand. He could only seek his followers from that tiny fraction of the human race that was living in Palestine in his own day. And even then, like us, he could not give himself to his friends as fully as he would have liked.

Similarly, he was hampered and held back from showing himself to be fully Son of God. So long as he remained subject to the earthly laws of space and time, of sin and death, he could not be with the Father. Full fellowship with God would have meant his translation out of this mortal condition to a state where he could no longer be attacked by temptation or limited to a changing and earthly existence.

But the more he endeavoured to preach God's message to men, the more did he become Son and Word. As he fought against the notion of giving up his mission, as he struggled against weariness and fear, as he tried to get God's message across as effectively as possible, or become more effectively God's Word to men, so he showed his love for God more fully as Son for Father. The closer he drew towards men, as Word, the closer did he draw, as Son, towards God.

This lifelong struggle at deepening his fellowship with the Father and mankind by trying to break free from the restrictions that are basic to our fallen condition could only succeed, not by his evading them or shirking them, but by his undergoing them. For he could not overcome, transfigure or transform them, for himself or for the rest of men, unless he first experienced them as fully as he could.

And this applied above all to death. For death sums up, as it were, those limitations that have tended to separate us from God and each other by isolating us completely in the grave and killing off all hope of any further relationship.

Jesus also experienced death as isolation and division. But he experienced it, too, as a way to the fulness of fellowship for which, all through his life on earth, he had been yearning and striving. Since, of all human beings, this man had been absolutely true to his vocation – had been both Son and Word as fully as his mortal condition would allow – then this man alone could not experience death as the end to all hope of a fuller union with God and man. Instead, if his vocation were to progress, if the relationship into which he had been born were to develop to its limits, if he were to be Son and Word as completely as was possible for a human being, then it could only be by his living on after death and in a new kind of way, freed for ever from the limiting laws of space and time and sin that had so hedged him in while on this earth.

It was in his resurrected state, then, that Jesus became fully what he was called to be from the first – Son and Word of the Father. The Godward and manward relationship into which he had been born had finally been brought to fulness and perfection. Jesus was now simultaneously at one with the Father and at one with the human race in a way not possible to him before.

Jesus and the Holy Spirit

And this brings us on to the very point that Roman Catholic theology came to discuss after dealing with Jesus' knowledge, and that is the fact of his *growth in grace*. By grace we mean the Holy Spirit as it was possessed by Jesus for his life on earth. By glory, we mean the gift of the Spirit made when Jesus had died to the life of earth.

Now, we have been talking of Jesus progressively living out his two-fold vocation until it reached its climax in his rising from the dead. But the gospels speak of this gradual deepening and activating of the double relationship precisely in terms of Jesus growing in grace, or in his possession of the Spirit.

As a child, when 'busy with my Father's affairs' (Luke 2:49), Jesus prepared himself for that further step in his vocational journey when he was to show his son-like love for God more thoroughly yet by preaching his word more tellingly and openly to man. In so schooling himself for his public ministry, he 'increased in wisdom, in stature, and in *favour* with God and man' (Luke 2:52).

Then, when he is baptised by John as the immediate prelude to taking up his preaching task, the Spirit descends like a dove upon him and the voice of God declares: 'You are my Son, the Beloved; my *favour* rests on you' (3:22).

Finally, when he displays his love for God to the uttermost, as Son, and at the same time shows forth God's love for men to the full, as Word, that is, by dying on the cross, that 'favour' or Spirit of the Father comes, not merely to grace him and give him added strength to combat his limitations, but in fact to glorify him.

The risen Christ is completely possessed and taken over by the Spirit. It is in the Spirit, according to scripture, that Christ is bound to the Father in an everlasting covenant of love; it is through the Spirit that the risen Christ draws close, in love, towards us; and it is by the power of this same Spirit, abiding in our hearts, that we are able to share in the love that Jesus displays towards God and the human race.

The Spirit, therefore, stands for the love that activates and intensifies all personal relationships. When we say that Christ is now filled with the Spirit, we mean that, as a human being, he is now fully able to give expression to that love for the Father to which, as Son, he was always dedicated, and to that love for men to which, as Word, he was called from the start.

When we go on to say that men of good will participate in the Spirit of the risen Lord, we mean that, whenever human beings love one another, or intensify those particular relationships with God and men to which they, too, were dedicated from their birth, they are in fact participating, however feebly, in the fulness of love that now wholly activates the relationship of Jesus as Son to the Father and as Word to us.

Two conclusions follow from all this.

Firstly, *grace is universal*. Since grace is the name we give to our partial sharing in the Spirit or love of Christ, then it seems that

Jesus must offer this Spirit to everyone without exception, since all are called to humanise and ripen their relationships with men until they develop into genuine love or fellowship. But wherever human beings love one another, wherever they strive to create human fellowship, there is the Spirit of Christ at work. And since this vocation to fellowship is a part of the basic human condition and always has been, then the grace of the Holy Spirit must have been offered and made available to all men, from the very beginnings of the race up to now, as it will be to the very end – yet in some way *because of* the Christ who-was-to-come.

Secondly, *it is misleading to speak of vertical and horizontal relationships*, the one with God and the other with mankind, as though the two were somehow in opposition. Jesus deepens his relationship of love towards God by deepening his love for men, draws closer to the Father in drawing closer to us, and *vice versa*. For it is only when he is completely glorified by the Spirit (that is, completely given in love to the Father since no longer held back by the restrictions of an earthly manner of existence) that he is able to send the Spirit upon men (that is, only because he is now fully united to the Father can he offer to men a share in that relationship of his until they, too, shall be completely taken over by it on being finally freed from the restrictions of an earthly existence). Thus men, too, will draw closer to God the closer they draw to their fellow human beings; the more they seek to rid themselves of all that hinders their full growth in fellowship, the deeper will they be participating in the love, or Spirit, that simultaneously binds Jesus completely to his Father and makes him offer himself completely to us.

Thus it is the fundamental law of Christianity that we can only love God by loving our neighbour. 'God is love,' says St John, 'and anyone who lives in love lives in God, and God lives in him' (1 John 4:16). But to live in love means, in fact, to love one's fellow human beings. 'Let us love *one another*, since love comes from God, and everyone who loves *is begotten by God and knows God*. Anyone who fails to love can never have known God, because God is love' (4:7, 8).

It is not everyone who cries out: 'Lord! Lord!', therefore, who will enter the kingdom of heaven, but those who do the will of the Father; and his will is that we should love him, worship him, serve him, by loving one another.

To love our neighbour is to love God. Conversely, to love God is to love our neighbour. Not that, the moment we stop doing things for other people or the minute we rest from our good works, we stop loving God. For love is a matter, not just of actions, but of the *attitude* that underlies them. Our love for God, which is our love for human-kind, is measured and determined by the attitude of open-heartedness and generosity of spirit that expresses itself in such deeds of loving service towards our neighbour.

The tension we may feel between the need for action and the call to contemplation will therefore be psychological rather than theological. We are communicating with God, entering into personal relationship with him, becoming more fully his children, the more we communicate with other people, enter into personal relationship with them, become a word from God to them by offering them a love in which they, too, will communicate with the Father in the Spirit of his Son.

We will obviously feel the need from time to time to recollect our thoughts, to meditate upon our efforts, to become more aware of and more grateful for this double relationship in Christ – and for the absolute priority of the transcendent God thus revealed as immanent among men. Indeed, such meditation will normally increase our desire to find a fuller freedom by entering more deeply upon this relationship, opening ourselves more generously towards God and our fellow men. If we are Christians or believers in a God, then we will call this operation *prayer*; if we remain unaware of the godly significance of what we are about we will call it by some other name; we will say we are 'thinking out our position' or 'taking stock of our lives'; but the reality of the increased double relationship will be the same.

Such activity, however, must not be thought of as somehow a surer contact with God since more vertical and more virtuous than our efforts at deepening our relationships with other people. Indeed, without such efforts, prayer would be at best meaningless and at worst hypocrisy or sham.

Chalcedon Re-stated

The question now arises as to whether our discussion on the vocation of Jesus does justice to traditional and orthodox belief concerning him. According to the council of Chalcedon, there are two complete and entire natures in Christ, the human and the divine, with neither nature being confused or mixed up with the other, but united only in that each belongs to the one divine person of the Word. This talk of 'person' and 'nature' reminds us, too, of the teaching of Nicaea that the divine nature of God exists in three divine persons.

The scholastics were later to elucidate and give greater precision to the rather vague meanings attached to the terms nature and person in the early councils, until they came to define a person as 'the termination of a rational nature'.

According to this definition, the *person* as such cannot act and is totally unable to do a single thing. Neither is the person at all conscious or aware of anything. Rather, the person is that which gives a unique and concrete existence to a rational nature. It is what makes a human being, for instance, this particular individual and not another. It is what differentiates man from man, making the one distinguishable from the other, though both possess a common human nature.

It is the *nature* that does all the acting. In a man, it is his human nature that thinks and feels and wills, that understands and is aware and conscious. But the activities of the nature are attributed to the non-acting, non-conscious person, since in every case the nature 'belongs', as it were, to this particular person and not to another.

Today, the opposite meaning generally attaches to the terms nature and person, and with it goes a deep misunderstanding and confusion about the traditional teaching on Christ and the Trinity.

By 'person' or 'personality', for instance, we generally mean today the 'ego', that is, the self as conscious of itself in becoming conscious of persons and things around it, according to its own psychic or emotional make-up. 'Human nature', on the other hand, we either regard as some abstract quality or label of human-ness that attaches to all acting, thinking, feeling human persons; or we think of it as specifically *my* nature, that which makes me different from everybody else. But in either case we are inclined to see human nature as something non-active and non-conscious.

In other words, what we usually call *person* the fathers of Chalcedon would have called *nature*, and what we generally speak of as *nature* they would have called *person*.

We have said that a human being derives his uniqueness from the fact that he exists as an individual with a unique set of relation-ships towards the rest of the race and hence towards God. But is not this precisely that non-active individualising principle that was covered, in the traditional teaching, by the term *person*?

We have also said that the human vocation is to live out and to activate those given relationships into which we are inserted by birth and which distinguish us from other people. In modern terms, we would say that we have to use our *personality* – that is, the temperament we have inherited through our particular deri-vation from the rest of the race – in order to enter, each in our own inimitable way, into real human fellowship with our neighbour and hence with God. In this way we form our char-acter, shape our life-style and mature as human beings. But is not this just what our predecessors in the faith meant by the work of our human *nature*, with its activities of thinking and feeling and willing?

If this is so, then to speak of Jesus as the person of the Son or Word of God existing in a human nature would be to speak of that special and unique relationship with God and men in which, as a human being, he existed from the start. What distinguishes this particular man from all others is that he alone exists as so open to God as to be a genuine communication of God to men. This is his vocation as a divine *person*.

This vocation must now be lived out in his human *nature*. By means of his human mind and heart and will and emotions, he must strive to make this nature conform to what he already is as a person – the Son and Word of God.

But if Jesus really is the Word and Son in human flesh and blood – that is, a man who exists precisely *as* God's final revelation of himself to man – then it follows that the person of the Word must be divine.

For Jesus announces to us that the best way to understand God is to think of his acting towards us like a father; but, in doing so, Jesus also reveals a Father-God who communicates to us, not just a message, but *himself*, giving himself to us in his Word. Jesus also reveals, and indeed opens out to us, the relationship of love that exists between the Father and himself as Son. This relationship of Son to Father he must live out as a human being until it is brought to perfection at his rising from the dead. And now, fully taken over, as a man, by the relationship of love that binds him to the Father, he extends that same relationship to us. He sends us the Spirit.

Jesus and the Trinity

In Jesus Christ, then, the deity is revealed as acting towards us in three different ways, offering itself to us in a threefold relationship – as Father, Son and Spirit. But if God thus *acts* in a triple manner, it can only be because he *exists* as triple.

For we have seen that the life of a human being – the activity of his human *nature* – is determined by the unique set of relationships into which he was born and in which he exists as a distinct individual – by his *person*. By analogy, therefore, we can say that God's threefold activity in our regard, his invitation to draw closer to him as Father by drawing closer to humanity in the Spirit or love of his risen Son, represents the living out in his divine nature of what he *is* personally. It is the 'vocation' of that nature to extend to us the threefold relationship that makes it unique, that 'personalises' it. God deals with us in a trinitarian way because he already exists as Trinity.

Jesus Christ reveals and communicates to us a God in three persons. This means, in turn, that the person of the Word, whom we meet in Jesus and who gives individual existence to his *human* nature, is also and at the same time one of the three terminations of the *divine* nature. God exists as Son or Word as well as Father and as Spirit. This Word must in consequence be giving individuality both to the divine and to this particular human nature. 'The Word' who was 'made flesh' is truly the Word that was 'with God in the beginning', that '*was* God' (John 1).

The Word therefore personalises two natures, one divine and the other human, so that both exist within the same unique set of relationships with God as Father and Spirit and with men. Thus the divine nature exists as Word in so far as this Word is the genuine reflection and communication of the Father and his love. And the humanity of Jesus exists as the same Word in that, through a full, complete and genuine human nature, the Father really gives himself in the love of the Spirit to the world of men. The two natures of Christ meet solely in that both exist as Word of God, proclaiming and radiating and communicating the love of the Father.

The relationship of Son or Word that is ever being lived by the divine nature is a relationship we see being progressively lived out, too, in the human nature of Jesus. And both sets of activity are attributable to the divine person of the Word. But it is only in this attribution that the two natures meet and are permanently united. Otherwise, they remain unmixed, unmingled, separate in their activities. We do not, then, see in Jesus a divine nature or set of activities proper to God but at work in human flesh, or divine actions taking place in human form. Though the works of Jesus as man may be called divine in that they are attributed to the divine Word that gives individual existence to his human nature, they remain nevertheless purely human activities. If the Word exists as a real man, then it must rightly be credited, not only with the activity of a God, but also with the activity of this man, and with his progress in wisdom and knowledge, with his gradual discovery about his mission in life, with his tiredness and hunger, sorrow and joy, loving-kindness and understanding.

This is also true of the miracles of Jesus. However we may explain these, however think of them as signs worked by the power of God, they do not imply that, at the miraculous moment, Jesus ceased from acting as a man and in a human way. The miracles of Jesus, like those of the saints, are performed through the agency of a nature that is neither more nor less than human, however stupendous and inexplicable the power that works through that nature might be.

To speak as we have been doing in terms of nature and person with regard to God, as indeed to treat the deity as a 'he' or as Father, Son and Spirit is to deal with the divinity in halting, limp, human analogies. Yet, if we are to say anything worthwhile or understandable about God at all, it must be in human terms and with reference to the human being, Christ Jesus. Furthermore, if we are to speak about the God revealed by this Jesus in words that will be relevant and meaningful today, we can only do so by trying faithfully to translate and re-interpret the data provided for us in the bible into modern thought-forms. But that means that we need constantly to refer to our forefathers' efforts at presenting the same biblical evidence in the terms of their own age and culture if our faith is to remain consistent with theirs. Once we have assured ourselves, however, that what we want to say about God today is all of a piece with what the fathers of Chalcedon and Nicaea were trying to say, then we need no longer worry about making use of their terminology. We can forget words like 'nature' and 'person' and plunge further forward with our discoveries about God.

But always we must begin with Jesus. For it is here supremely that we meet God in human terms and on our own ground. A deity who must remain otherwise largely incomprehensible thus communicates himself to us as a God who is *with* us and *for* us, drawing us all the time, as we seek to enter into communication with other human beings, into communion with himself, so that we meet him as Father in the Spirit of his Son.

And the knowledge of this God-revealing Jesus comes to us

through the bible and the preaching of the Christian Church. So that it is to the community of Christians and to its witness through the ages that we must turn if we would discover Jesus as Word of the Father and source of his Spirit.

But if, as we have claimed, this Spirit, or the love that activates the relationship between Father and Son in the deity and that glorifies the human nature of the Son made man, is in fact available universally; if all who strive to be loving and open towards others are in reality already living by the Spirit of Christ and are thus opening themselves up to fellowship with the Father; then what is the point of knowing about Jesus or of attaching oneself to his Church? Why not be content with an agnostic humanism?

To try and answer this question, we must take a fresh look at the role of the Church today, and at the significance for the modern world of her preaching the gospel and her celebrating the liturgy.

3

THE NEW TRIUMPHALISM

Two Affirmations of Vatican II

VATICAN II was meant to spell out the end of triumphalism. At least, so many of the fathers thought as they
rose, one by one, to condemn the idea of the Church as a
great super-power with its heart set on the political domination
of the earth, or as some big-business corporation bent on winning
worldly prestige. The Church was meant to be the servant of the
world, they declared, and not its master.

Even at the time of the Council, however, and more increasingly since, this role of the Church as the servant of men came to
be interpreted in two divergent ways, according to the manner
in which theologians tried to reconcile two very important but
apparently conflicting statements made by Vatican II.

1. *The Church is the sacrament of Christ's saving presence in the
   world:* hence the Church is in some way necessary for salvation
   (Constitution on the Church);

2. *The grace of Christ is universal:* since every man who follows
   his conscience will be saved (Decree on Religious Liberty).

Schillebeeckx and 'Anonymous Christianity'

Schillebeeckx, to whom goes the distinction of having prepared
the way for the Council's teaching on the Church as sacrament
by his thorough-going treatment of the subject in *Christ the
Sacrament*,[1] managed to harmonise the two doctrines in this way.

Jesus Christ is the 'primordial sacrament' who, in his life, death
and resurrection, was not only a *sign* to men that God loved them

[1] Sheed and Ward. 1963.

and longed for their salvation, but was also an *effective* sign, in that he was a sign that actually brought about and made available the very salvation that he proclaimed. And a sign that effects what it signifies is precisely what we mean by a sacrament.

Since the risen Lord is now a sign to us no longer, having been removed from the range of our senses, he has bequeathed that sacramental function to the visible Christian community, the Church. In other words, the Church is a *sign* of Christ's enduring presence among men, and of his continuing offer of salvation. And it is an *effective* sign, since, through its witness and its worship, it actually makes this salvation of Christ present in our world of space and time. The Church, too, is a genuine sacrament.

This sacrament-Church is also a servant-Church: that is to say, it performs the service of handing on to mankind throughout history the saving grace that Jesus won by rising from the dead. But the Church itself can only transmit grace to men because of its own sacraments, and above all because of the eucharist which is its indispensable source of grace so that, without it, the Church could not exist.

This grace that flows from the liturgy into the Church and from the Church into the world has two main effects. First of all, it creates unity. All those who receive the Spirit of Christ – that is, all who genuinely try to love and serve other people – are bound in fellowship with God the Father, with all good Christians, and indeed with all good men and women everywhere.

All who possess the Spirit belong to the Church considered as a *fellowship*. This fellowship-Church is consequently much wider than the Church considered as a *sacrament*, and contains in its ranks all well-meaning men and women even if, through no fault of their own, they have never heard of Christ or find themselves unable to believe in him. In that case they will be *anonymous* Christians.

The second effect of grace is that, because it comes from the Church and from the sacraments of the Church, it draws all who receive it – all, that is (including the 'anonymous Christians') who belong to the fellowship-Church – into full, visible membership of the sacrament-Church, and to baptism and the eucharist.

But this sacrament-Church, while truly present in all the Christian Churches, subsists most fully in the Roman Catholic Church. There is some element, however much hidden or mis-understood, of the visible ecclesiastical organisation set up origin-ally by Christ that other Churches lack but that the Roman Church has retained. Consequently, grace is leading all other Christians into full visible communion with the Church of Rome.

As sacrament, the Church will ultimately pass away; as fellow-ship she will endure forever. Then, at the end of time, all those good people who have never belonged to the Church as visible organisation will find that they have belonged to the fellowship-Church all along. They will be no longer anonymous but explicit in their Christianity, and members of that full and perfect fellow-ship of all the blessed that will be the Church in glory.

But the Church will not only emerge the winner in the end; for, if grace is really leading all men here and now into visible membership of the sacrament-Church, then it would seem highly likely that this purpose will one day be actually achieved on this earth. And then the Church, which now might appear hidden and humble, will emerge as triumphant even in time and space, for it will have become co-terminous with the whole human race, or at least with all the men of good will in the race.

As fellowship, the Church even now is the human race at its best, since all the best of the race are even now in the Church. And one day this fact will be made obvious, explicit and visible to all in the Church as sacrament. Thus, of the two communities, that of the Church and that of the race, it is the Church com-munity that is primary and all-important, with the human community very much its subordinate.

Furthermore, visible membership of the sacrament-Church, and particularly of the Roman communion, would seem to give men a spiritual advantage over their fellows. Whereas the state of the 'anonymous Christian' is precarious and that of the non-Catholic Christian ambiguous, the Roman Catholic both knows with greater clarity what he is about and is also aided far more fully by the grace of the sacraments. His status is thus privileged, his way to heaven made more smooth than that of other men.

This is, I think, a fair summary of the thought of Schillebeeckx, not as it is now, but as it stood at the time of Vatican II and as it has come to be *under*stood by others subsequently. Karl Rahner, on the other hand, saw things rather differently. Even during the Council, he was writing of the Church as being in a diaspora situation (scattered – as the Jews were after the temple was destroyed). And this idea of *the Church of the diaspora* has become the keystone to a whole new understanding of the Church that has grown up since Vatican II.

Karl Rahner and the Diaspora-Church

Rahner had long been asserting, in contrast to Schillebeeckx, that, while the grace of Christ was truly universal and offered to everybody, yet that grace did not always come to men by way of the Church or of her sacraments. In other words, grace did not inevitably draw the non-Christian to Church membership, to baptism and the eucharist.

He came to this conclusion because he rejected the notion of extending the Church beyond the bounds of the visible ecclesial organisation. In other words, only those who belonged to the Church as sacrament could also belong to her as fellowship. For them, the Holy Spirit did indeed come through the mediation of the Church and of her sacraments, but even in their case not exclusively so. Grace was also ministered to them through their everyday dealings with their neighbours in the world. Since to love is to allow the Spirit of the risen Lord to activate one's given relationships with other people and thus to be overtaken by grace, it follows that, whenever a human being leads another on to acts of love and service, he becomes a source of grace to his fellow. But, if we are to restrict the Church to its visible membership, then the grace-ful encounters that all men, Christian or not, are called upon to make with their neighbours can hardly be called ecclesial or sacramental, since they do not originate in the Church or in her liturgical worship.

Could this grace be called ecclesial and sacramental, however, in the sense that, though originating from within the human and not the ecclesial community, it nevertheless leads those who receive it into the visible Church and to her sacraments?

Again, Rahner would deny this. For the facts would seem to indicate quite otherwise. Statistically, Christianity is, after all, on the decline. Mainly a white man's religion for over a thousand years, it is losing ground not only in the mission lands but even at home. In Europe, more people forsake Christianity than join it every year. The traditionally Catholic countries are themselves feeling the pinch, while theological colleges and seminaries, convents and vicarages fall empty and are put up for sale.

At the same time, the growth of national awareness in the emerging nations has meant that their vast populations are finding a new pride in their own native cultures and religions and a growing distrust for things that seem white and European in origin, and thus smack of colonialism. This mood in part accounts for the great revival of Mohammedanism and Hinduism in parts of Africa and India at the present moment, and the corresponding difficulty Christian missionaries find in preaching the gospel in those areas.

Furthermore, the drastic dwindling of the Christian Church's relative importance in the world is inevitable when one sees how rapidly the non-Christian east is outstripping the once-Christian west even numerically and in terms of the population explosion. We are told that the population of China alone will outnumber the combined present populations of Europe, Russia, Africa, India and north and south America within half a century!

Political power, too, is heading east. No longer is Europe the mistress of the world, while, of our new masters, the U.S. is being constantly challenged by the U.S.S.R. and the U.S.S.R. by China, with the sleeping giants of Africa and India waiting in the wings for their turn to take the stage. The prestige that the Church once enjoyed in the world, and indeed that she still largely enjoys, is about to fade swiftly away.

To an outside observer, the Church must look more and more

like a white minority religious grouping of decreasing interest
and importance. Does that mean that Christianity is failing, that
the Church is, in fact, dying out? Will she never convert the
world, but must she be content with a lessening number of
adherents? Or is her task something different?

Karl Rahner would say that it is. He would claim that her role
is to be, quite simply, the Church of the diaspora. In the days of
its birth, the Christian community was neither a society to be
respected nor a force to be reckoned with. Rather, it was a hidden,
humble, despised organisation with no pretensions to grandeur
at all. Yet this Church of the New Testament is held up before
us as the model of what the Church should be in every age.

The Church today will therefore be losing nothing essential if
she loses her prestige in the world. Indeed, she will be gaining.
For she will be returning to the New Testament model, becoming
once more a Church thinly scattered among men, a Church that
most of them will perhaps hardly notice. But she will be a Church
dedicated, not to regaining her former earthly glories, but to
serving mankind in a lowly and obscure kind of way, like the
mustard-seed men tread underfoot or the piece of yeast that works
all unnoticed in the great mass of dough.

For it is not the main task of the Church to preach the gospel,
but to help the whole human race grow together in love. Paul's
famous saying is as true of the Christian community as it is of the
individual Christian: 'If I have all the eloquence of men or of
angels, but speak without love, I am simply a gong booming or a
cymbal clashing' (1 Cor. 13:1).

The Church, therefore, must make it her first duty to be present
wherever men are striving to live in harmony, to create fellowship, to eradicate all those evils that at present divide the human
race. Through her members she must be eager to co-operate and
work alongside all men of good will, no matter what their creed,
culture or political beliefs, to help bring about one single community of mankind, a community that the Church understands
as the kingdom of heaven.

Meanwhile, the diaspora-Church will still have the duty of

preaching the gospel until the coming of this kingdom. She will not do so, however, with an eye to converting the world. For she must recognise, first, that only God, by his grace, can call individuals to Church membership and, second, that God has given us no guarantee that he does, in fact, issue his call to all or even to most of the human race at any given period of its history.

On the contrary, the parables of the yeast and the mustard-seed to which we have already referred would seem to imply the reverse. Rather, the work upon which the Church is primarily engaged, that of helping to establish the kingdom of God, will always seem as small and insignificant as the seed and the leaven. But the end product, the kingdom when established, will be as wide and high and all-embracing as a great tree, as whole and complete as a round and swelling loaf.

In other words, Jesus is putting before us, in either case, two pictures, the one of the kingdom as it now is, and the other of the kingdom as it will be at the last. He makes no further connection between the two, however. He does not say that the work of establishing the kingdom will grow steadily throughout history like a seed growing into a tree, or that, like yeast, it will gradually permeate the dough. He gives us, therefore, no kind of assurance that the Church will progress visibly, either in numbers or indeed in holiness, until the kingdom is finally established.

Neither does he identify the kingdom as seed or yeast with the Church. In fact, it is only the men and women of good will in both communities, the human and the ecclesial, who are at work on this enterprise of making the kingdom a reality. This is the first duty of all human beings, therefore, whether Christian or not – to help the race achieve community.

However, Rahner would go on to insist that the work of the human community, a work in which the lesser community of the Church is meant to take part and co-operate, is only made possible because of the existence of the smaller Christian community. In other words, the universal availability of grace is a fact because of the very existence of the Church in the world. The Holy Spirit that manifests itself wherever human beings truly enter into fellowship with one another, and that may or may not come to them through the Church community and through its sacraments, is nevertheless only present, from the beginning of time to its end, because of Jesus and the community of Christians that he first gathered round him and that perpetuates itself down the ages. Thus the Church may be destined always to be rejected or ignored by the majority of men. She may be heading, in our own days, for a darker obscurity. She may soon become much more hidden and humble than she has ever been since first given official backing by Constantine over fifteen hundred years and more ago. Her service to mankind may go forever unrecognised and unrewarded by the world. But it will still be a service that is absolutely vital, since without it the kingdom could never be established and the work of good men towards that end would be deprived of its value and meaning as a manifestation of the Spirit.

These basic intuitions of Karl Rahner were disturbing and uncomfortable to many people at the time of the Council, whereas Schillebeeckx's views appeared much more open, progressive and hopeful. Rahner seemed to delight in painting a gloomy picture of the future of Christianity; he reduced the Church, it was felt, almost to insignificance; and above all he failed to show exactly why this poor, diminished Church should be so necessary for man's salvation.

Concealed Triumphalism

But then, as his followers began to expand and explain Rahner's original ideas, so they uncovered an unwitting triumphalism in the more popular explanation.

First, as men like Kung and Tillman were asking, is it not arrogant to claim all men of good will for the Church of Christ, even if they positively reject the Christian gospel? Is it not insulting and indeed a misuse of language to tell the pious Muslim or Hindu or agnostic humanist that he is, all the time and despite any protest he might make, an 'anonymous Christian'? How would we Christians react if we were likewise told that, by living up to our calling, we were in fact being good Hindus or Muslims and contributing to the growth of those 'churches', without our knowing it and against our will?

True, the good Christian is linked with all other good men in that all are living by the same Spirit of Jesus. But just as it is triumphalist to go on and declare that the best of the race is consequently 'in' the Church (since all who genuinely love, and who therefore share in the Spirit, are part of the Church as a fellowship) so it is triumphalist to assume that all men are called into full and visible membership of that Church when both the gospel and the history of Christianity would seem to point in quite the other direction.

It is trumphalist, too, to suppose that the community that is to come will in fact *be* this self-same Church existing in her final state of heavenly glory. Though we may speak of the glorified community as 'the Church triumphant', this Church-of-the-future will not simply come to pass as the continuation of a Church that already, here on earth, includes all men of good will within its grasp. This is to make the Church, both on earth and in heaven, not only the most important but in fact the only real community. For, in this view, wherever we find human community growing between men, and whatever the name we care to call this developing society, it is the fellowship-Church that in fact we are looking at, albeit in disguise.

Rahner's view rescues the race from this next-to-nothingness by recognising that true human fellowship, though always the work of the Holy Spirit, can and does exist within the human race but outside the community of the Christian Church. Both societies, that of the Church and that of mankind in general, are working towards the establishment of a single community of the future that will be the fulfilment and perfection of each, while, in that work, it is the human race that is primary, with the Church as a lesser community included within it and completely at its service.

Though Christian and non-Christian are together working for the same end, does the Christian have any other advantage over his brother beyond the fact that he knows more clearly where he and the race are going and thus lives his life in the joyful confidence that, however hopeless things might appear, the kingdom is nevertheless surely on its way? Karl Rahner himself felt that the call to Christianity (and, among Christians, the call to Roman Catholicism, since the Roman Church in some way retains all those institutional elements Christ gave his Church at its inception) is a further call to privilege in that the Christian (and especially the Roman Catholic) is able to find salvation more readily and easily than the rest of men.

But this point, too, is being challenged as a last relic of the triumphalist temper that Rahner has done so much to exorcise from Roman Catholic theology.

Certainly, the Christian Church is necessary for salvation. Certainly it is the indispensable sacrament of God's love for humanity. But in this sense.

Mankind is and always has been under the grace of Christ, so that wherever you find human love there you in fact find the reign of his Spirit penetrating human hearts. The Church's particular task is to *represent* the human race and its graced condition before the eyes of God and the world. Its job is to *be* that race in miniature, and to make the true state of that race both *obvious* and *explicit*.

The Church is a gathering of sinners. It is made up of evil-doers and is riddled with wickedness. Its members bicker and quarrel and fight and live isolated little lives, cut off from each other by self-interest and self-concern. At the same time, the Church is a gathering of saints. For, despite its corruption, the Church strives to defeat and overcome the sin that threatens always to split it up into factions and classes, and tries instead to become more truly one, more fully a community, more really a family. But the Church also goes on to testify to its belief that Jesus is risen from the dead, that the Spirit of his resurrection is available to men, and that it is by the power of this Spirit that the sin of the Church is being overcome and genuine fellowship established. The Church's community spirit is the *Holy* Spirit.

And this is really what the race is like as a whole. It, too, is full of corruption. Its harmony is constantly threatened by the self-interest of nations or classes or parties. Prejudice and exploitation lead it into violence and warfare. Yet, at the same time, the race is being drawn into brotherhood. For men are all the time at work in its ranks trying to get the warring factions to live in peace, trying to educate people out of prejudice, trying to create just societies where men can live more human lives, freed from the fear of being exploited and enslaved by their fellows. In other words, the sin in the world that is the factor of division among men is being opposed by the Spirit of the risen Christ, the factor of unity that draws men together in love and the guarantee that sin shall finally be no more when the community of the kingdom of heaven has been fully achieved.

This is the Christian reality that underlies what is going on at present in the world and to which the Church of Christ is meant to bear explicit and clear witness on behalf of an unheeding race.

The Purpose of the Church

Why God should want a little religious group to act as the whole world's representative we cannot say – except that this is the way salvation seems to work. Just as Israel stood before the Lord as representing a larger mankind searching for redemption; as Jesus the man won new life for the rest of his race by acting as their representative before his Father; so the Church of Jesus Christ, as a miniaturisation of that race, openly acknowledges him as the Word of God on behalf of the vast majority of men who never have and never will believe – and in doing so somehow makes their salvation a real possibility.

The Christian Church represents the race; but it is meant to represent the *whole* race. The grace of God, therefore, calls, not each and every human being to membership of the Church, but *representatives, delegates* from every nation and class and culture. That is why the gospel must still be preached through the ages and in all the world's imagined corners – so that those whom the Spirit is prompting to come into the visible ecclesial community might understand and respond to the call. The Church is universal and catholic, then, in that, both, she is meant to give a telling witness to the fact that salvation is being offered to all mankind, and also that she must adequately represent the human community and take all that is good from every culture and society into her system if her witness is to be really impressive.

We have established that the Church represents the race and makes explicit its real condition before God. But what is the point of this representative function? However helpful it may be for the Christian's understanding of the state of man, can we reasonably go on from there to assert that it is necessary for the world's salvation?

Though Karl Rahner himself felt the force of this question, it is his followers who have begun to provide something like a convincing reply.

They do so by reminding us how it is that God saves man, that is, by *revealing* himself. Thus he saves the majority of men by making himself known to them in some way through the things of this world and in the fellow members of their race. To respond with knowledge and love to the needs of other people is to have the beginnings of a faith in God and of eternal life. It is to receive his Holy Spirit.

But the saving Word or revelation of God that is made to men by means of the human community is as yet not heard clearly or understood consciously. God reveals himself more plainly, however, in the great religions of the world, and in such a way that those who try to live up to their religious convictions will find their salvation in systems that explain more clearly the relationship with God that is set up whenever one tries to love one's neighbour. Among these religions, Judaism believes that God revealed himself above all as a saviour-God by actually rescuing the Hebrews from their Egyptian bondage.

But God's revelation of himself find its fullest expression, according to Christian belief, in the man Christ Jesus who, as the Word made flesh and by his rising from the dead, both disclosed the Father to his disciples as a God who saves from sin and death, and also brought about the very salvation that he thus proclaimed.

Salvation, therefore, comes about by *revelation*. But revelation is made up, not simply of God's activity in making himself known to man, but also of man's responding. The two elements, a Word from God and man's acceptance of that Word in faith, are both so vital to the idea of revelation that, if one of them is missing, nothing has in fact been revealed. If God 'revealed' himself to the empty air, for instance, or spoke his Word into the void, he could not be said to be revealing or speaking in any real and accepted sense at all.

Revelation is a communication that God makes *to people*. And it is a communication *that saves*. Now, we have already seen that it is part of man's present condition on this earth to be both fallen and redeemed, open at the same time to temptation and to grace. And this grace, which is his partial sharing in the Spirit of the risen Lord, has always been fully available to the human race.

For what is this saving grace of God? It is man's participation in the love that now binds Jesus completely to his Father and to mankind. It is to be known, therefore, by its fruits, so that, wherever one finds a genuine human love at work, *there*, one may say, is salvation, *there* is the Spirit. But this kind of love is as old as the human race. At any stage in its history, there have been men and women who have tried to live for others, to devote themselves to the service of their fellow human beings, to foster fellowship, brotherhood and community among men.

And this is only to be expected. For God, who is the Father *of all*, and Jesus, whom he sent as Saviour and Redeemer *of all*, can hardly prefer the men and women born A.D. to those who existed B.C., and give the former more chance of salvation and a fuller offer of grace than the latter, merely because of the accident of their date of birth. Nevertheless, the grace that has always been fully offered to man throughout his history was won for him at a particular time in that history by the life, death and resurrection of Jesus.

Salvation, therefore, is historical in that it has been accomplished on our behalf by the historical personage of Jesus Christ, and in that it is a condition that has always been fully open to man throughout his history. But we have already said that God saves mankind by revealing himself. Thus, if salvation is historical, then revelation must be historical too.

In other words, salvation has only been present and available to man at any time in his story because God has been constantly revealing himself to man. But if revelation requires, not only the uttering of a self-disclosing Word by God, but also the acceptance of that Word by *somebody* at least and as representing humanity at large, it follows that, throughout human history, there must always have been men and women who have acknowledged the Word of God explicitly on behalf of the rest of the race. The salvation of God has only been *fully available* to human beings historically because the revelation of God has always been *freely made* to them historically.

Again, this revelation is historical in that it is a partial and progressive disclosure. God only gradually reveals himself more plainly to mankind or makes known to men more explicitly the nature of the offer of salvation he is ever making to them until the coming of the Word made flesh. This means that, at any moment in the race's history, there must always have been people who have recognised and believed in the revealing Word of God as openly, plainly and explicitly as it was being offered. Unless this were so, then not only would revelation have ceased to progress until its fulfilment in Christ, but also, without the historical continuance of a community of believers, salvation would have ceased from being opened out to the race.

The progressive revelation of God thus implies a progressive understanding and acknowledgement of God's Word by a group of human beings throughout history. And, since revelation is salvation, that group of human beings makes salvation possible to the rest of the world at any given moment, and also gives saving value to other and less complete revelations that are being made to other groups of men at that particular time.

The Hebrews were the chosen people of God, not in so far as

they were privileged to receive a more genuine and effective offer of salvation than other people, but in that the offer of saving grace that God was making to the Egyptians, the Philistines, the Persians, Greeks or Romans and that some of these dimly understood, was only made possible because of the faith of Israel, whose service it was to make salvation obtainable by all the men of their day through their own acceptance of the Word of God as far as it had been given at that particular moment in time.

But the Word of God is only given its final expression in the man Christ Jesus, who is the fulness of salvation because he is also the fulness of revelation. But if Jesus is the saving Word in virtue of whose coming the lesser revelations made by God in the past had their own saving worth, then he himself can only be God's revelation (and therefore salvation) for men if there are individuals who will accept him as Son of God, believe in him as Saviour of the world, hear him as Word of the Father.

It was because of the existence of a Christian community, explicitly believing in Jesus on behalf of the larger human community, that he was able to bring salvation to the men of his own day. But since salvation is to be offered continually until the end of human history, then that community of believers we call the Christian Church must go on existing, go on acknowledging God's Word, from age to age. Thus the existence of the historical Church ensures the presence of the Spirit to a world embedded in history until Christ comes again.

To be called by God to membership of this little minority group is to be called, then, not to a privileged or more genuine offer of salvation, but to the performance of a special and indeed indispensable form of service – that of making the salvation that Jesus won for everybody actually available to the men and women of this particular age. Thus the human efforts towards creating community, the understanding of God presented by the various philosophies, ideologies and religions, all these partial hearings of the Word of God are made means of grace for men because of the Church's existence here and now and at every moment of human history from the days of Jesus to the end of time.

And even within the Christian Church, the Roman Catholic has received a call, not to a state that is privileged above that of his fellow-Christians, but to a form of Christianity in which, basically, the Word of God, so he believes, is to be heard more fully and clearly than by his brethren. Mere Church membership gives no guarantee of spiritual favour and benefit above what is given to the rest of men, therefore. It imparts no right to worldly honour and prestige, nor any assurance that the whole human race is destined to join the Roman Catholic ranks. Instead, Christian allegiance is a form of service that is absolutely necessary here and now, since, without it, man's condition as fallen and yet redeemed and under the grace of God would cease to be a fact.

The call to belong to the Church is a call to help the Christian community represent the human race at this particular point in time by responding explicitly on its behalf to the Word of God. Not only is it true that not everybody is called to this particular form of service, but Yves Congar would go further and state quite categorically that the majority of men are definitely *not* called to become Christians, much less Catholics. In other words, he would say, Christianity is not the ordinary, but an *extra*-ordinary way of salvation. Most men are saved through their attempts to live decent human lives, through their conscientious ideological or political beliefs, through their particular forms of religion and culture. These are the guidelines within which their love for the human race will be drawn out and understood and pursued.

How the extra-ordinary call, the vocation to membership of the Church, comes about, and the way the Church's own vocation as the representative of the human race is meant to be lived out, these are questions we will look at more closely in the following chapter.

4

THE WORD OF REVOLUTION

ALTHOUGH THE theology underlying Vatican II's description of Jesus as sacrament speaks of him as the sacrament of *man's encounter with God*, and though the Council itself talked of the Church as being both sacrament of Christ and also *sign of the unity of the entire human race*, in fact the tone of the documents on divine revelation and on the Church tends to emphasise the free initiative taken by God in either case rather than man's own free response.

This is understandable when one remembers the special pre-occupation of the council, which set out to stress that revelation, for instance, was more than God's proposing certain doctrines for our acceptance, but rather the mystery of his complete giving of himself to us in a man, Christ Jesus. Similarly, it wanted to show that the Church was something more than the association of those who believed in Jesus into one organised society whose officials formulated the doctrines God had revealed, but was again first and foremost a mystery coming freely from the Father and given to us in Jesus his Son.

However, the need has since been recognised of bringing out more clearly the indispensable – though admittedly secondary – part man himself has to play in both of these mysteries. Gabriel Moran in particular has reminded us how true this is of the whole process of revelation. For God can only speak his full and self-revealing Word to us because he has first spoken it to the man Jesus. The Word did not become incarnate in Jesus by the simple process of the Father as it were commandeering and requisitioning a particular piece of human flesh and blood through which to make himself more clearly known. Rather, Jesus was only Word of God to us because he himself always received that Word as fully as he possibly could in his human nature, that is as a human being and in a perfectly human way. So deeply does he hear the Word, indeed, that he actually *personifies* it – he *is* the Word in the form of man.

And he accepts that Word on our behalf, so that whenever we, too, hear and receive it as coming to us in Christ, our own response will be nothing less than a participation and entering into the response made by the humanity of Jesus.

Jesus the man responds in two ways – in charity and in faith. He loves and is aware, that is to say, of the God who offers himself to him with a love and awareness that is as full as it can possibly be according to the stage of development of Jesus' human heart and mind and consciousness. Though always fully open to the Father as a human being, it is his vocation to live out and experience what it means to be Word and Son of the Father in a developing, human way that is not complete until he is raised from the dead to behold God face to face in glory.

When we, therefore, come to know and love the same God and Father by accepting and believing in his Word made flesh, that human response of ours will in fact be a sharing in the very knowledge and love (again according to our own capacities and depending upon the stage reached by our own physical and psychic development) with which the manhood of Christ receives that Word.

The Church, furthermore, is that group of human beings which accepts Jesus as Word of the Father on behalf of the rest of the race. That is not to say that no one else can or does receive him. As we have seen, all who open their hearts to their fellow human beings in love are in fact opening themselves up to this Word. But they do not always know it. They are not conscious or aware of the mystery of that which they receive.

The Christian community, therefore, performs the service of accepting consciously – but not necessarily more lovingly – what other men accept with a less clear knowledge. She is a believing before she is a proclaiming Church.

And this is not to be wondered at if she is really sign and sacrament of Christ. For if Jesus saves us by first *accepting* the Word of God on our behalf so as to *be* that Word in human form, then the Church, too, must continue his work by accepting that Word in faith before she can preach it and witness to it. Just as, without Jesus opening himself up to become the Word in the very depths of his humanity, that Word could never have been made flesh for our salvation, so, unless the Church throughout history and on behalf of the human race acknowledged Jesus as Word, then his salvation would not be available to the rest of mankind here and now.

Thus God's call and man's reply together make up the one revelation of the Father that we find in Jesus Christ himself and in his Church. In this sense, it is true to say that the Church is indeed both sacrament of Christ and sacrament of man. That is, she not only stands for and makes plain and evident in human history the salvation offered to mankind by God through Jesus; she also stands for and makes plain man's reply to that offer, again in the reply made by Jesus. And since her function is truly sacramental, she not only represents this two-fold action, she also makes it possible and brings it about. By her very presence in this world as sign, she makes the offer of salvation from God and the reply of mankind that were both brought about in Christ valid and available and open to the whole of humanity.

But how does she represent the human race as accepting salvation? By being basically a brotherhood, one people united in the love of the Holy Spirit. In other words, the Word of God which she hears openly and explicitly has the effect of making her a single community. But in this she is only making manifest what the same Word, though largely unrecognised, is also achieving in the human race as a whole. The Church, called by the Word into one brotherhood, is meant to stand for humanity as called into the brotherhood of man.

But this Word of God is also destructive. It is a two-edged

sword that builds up but also tears down. If the Church is to live up to her vocation, if she is to obey that Word herself and live as one united community, then she must be prepared to eradicate and overthrow all that endangers or prevents full brotherhood among her members and between them and the world. In so doing, she will be reflecting what the human race at large must also do if it is to be formed by the Word into one family. All men, whether Christian or not, must be prepared to protest against anything that threatens human community. 'Every type of discrimination, whether social or cultural, whether based on sex, race, colour, social condition, language or religion is to be overcome and eradicated as contrary to God's intent' (Constitution on the Church in the Modern World, art. 29).

It is for this reason that theologians today are beginning to think of the Word of God as a Word of revolution. Far from shrinking from the idea of revolt, protest, dissent or the rocking of the boat, they are coming round to seeing such activity as at times the duty of the Christian as of any honest man.

By revolution, however, they are not primarily or necessarily thinking of armed rebellion, with the rumbling of the tumbrils and the fall of the guillotine. They will only go on to discuss the relative merits and de-merits of violent and non-violent revolutions when they have decided what they mean by revolution in the first place.

Generally speaking, a revolution begins with a prophetic vision, with an idealised picture of what human society could be like, and then goes on to compare the dream with the present reality. In so doing, it becomes clear that the vision will never become a fact unless the shape of society is somehow turned upside down, spun right around, shaken to its very roots.

True revolution, therefore, starts in the hearts of individuals, and lies in the demand that it makes for their *conversion* to the deal of human brotherhood in some form or other. As Pope Paul said in Populorum Progressio, 'this road towards a greater humanity requires effort and sacrifice; but suffering itself, accepted for the love of our brethren, favours the progress of the entire human family'.

The conversion of men and nations is required so that *renewal* might take place. As the term implies, renewal, though it has its eyes fixed on the future, must also keep looking back into the past. For any vision of what mankind might become should be based upon what he has shown himself to be in his previous history, with all his successes and mistakes, his capabilities and limitations, his unhappiness and his hope for a better world.

If the Church's special service is to make explicit the fact that God's Word is gathering together the whole human race into one brotherhood by the power of the glorifying Spirit of love, and since that Word is one that speaks of revolution, conversion and renewal, what is the Christian reality behind these terms to which the Christian community must bear witness?

First of all, the Church makes plain her belief that to turn towards one's fellow human beings in love is in fact to turn towards God, in and through a Christ who is himself present in those we meet and serve. An encounter with the poor is an encounter with Jesus in that he wants, through us, to serve the poor. To relieve their poverty, of whatever kind it may be, is to meet Christ, for it is as though what one is doing to the poor, for good or ill, one were doing directly to him.

To obey the Word of God as we hear it in the human community by responding to our neighbour's need for our love is the basic form of conversion, of that change of heart and continuous revolution in our ways of thinking and acting to which we are all of us called. Religious conversion to God and to the Christian faith merely expresses and explains the true reality that underlies this process so that, without it, conversion in any Christian sense would be impossible. Our turning towards God by entering into the Christian community is meant to make explicit that deeper turning towards God that took place without our fully knowing it when we began to love others and so make our entry into the family of man.

Real conversion demands renewal. To the individual Christian as to the Church as a whole, this renewal will consist in a more thorough application of the directives of the gospel. Christian renewal is thus meant to be *radical* in the sense that it looks back to the *roots* of its faith, to the original witness of the Word made flesh, in order to see how that Word would have his followers live today. The Church will then try to renew itself in the light of the gospels so as to be the better able to help the whole of mankind consolidate and usher in the fulness of God's reign in the perfect fellowship in the Spirit that is to come.

In doing so, the Church makes it clear that all human efforts at a personal and communal renewal that are genuinely radical will in fact be concerned with the better putting into operation of the basic command of Jesus that we should love one another. In fact, the Church goes on to say, such efforts help establish a brotherhood that is nothing less than the kingdom of God.

The Word of God is a Word, then, of conversion. It calls upon men to turn back lovingly to their God, but goes on to point out that this return will only be sincere if it results in a turning in greater love towards the human community. Any renewal of their relationship with God must include a genuine attempt to renew their relationships with their fellow human-beings and to re-shape and re-structure their society whenever the need arises so that such relationships may be more readily possible between all the individuals who make up that society. The Word demands both personal and social upheaval – and it demands it *soon*. Now is the acceptable time, and no other. The moment of hearing is the moment for replying.

And this is evident from the witness of the written Word of God. The bible indeed might well be called the revolutionary manifesto of the Christian. Take, to begin with, the central event of the Old Testament, the story of the exodus. This starts with a call to conversion and ends with a massive act of civil disobedience.

Moses hears the Word of Yahweh from out of the burning bush, telling him to take off his shoes in reverence before the Lord. Later, through Moses, Yahweh also reveals himself to the Hebrews as a God who wants their worship. But the Word demands more than mere external rites, the baring of feet and the shedding of blood. If their worship is to be sincere, Moses and the other Hebrews must show it by their actions. They must do something here and now to change their world if they are to become the People of God.

Moses himself must go at once to Pharaoh and demand the release of his kinsfolk. The rest of the Hebrews must follow Moses out into the desert, where they will learn that, to show their love for Yahweh, they must love their fellow Hebrews as themselves. Thus God calls for revolution, both in the hearts of his people and in their attitudes to himself and to one another. He is no mere cultic deity, satisfied with lip-service and ceremonial.

The Jews thus came to understand the passover of their forebears as a mighty act of rebellion against the powers that be, a great freedom march out of slavery and into the Promised Land, and one that was commanded and supported by God himself. The Hebrews in fact were dissidents who, at Yahweh's instigation, had risen up against Egyptian exploitation and re-formed themselves out of the disorganised rabble they had been into a unified nation.

But the Word of God, coming to them with such shattering consequences through Moses the great prophet, was to be heard time and again in their later history through other prophets, and each time as a further call to revolution. Looking back to the original exodus experience, the prophets saw in it the blue-print of how the People of God ought to live in the future as compared with the way they were actually living now.

For, as they gave up their nomadic way of life and settled down in Palestine, they began to fix up and establish for themselves a pattern of living very much at odds with the requirements of God's Word, since it was based on self-seeking rather than on brotherhood. The rulers and the rich sought further power and wealth, the high priests and professional holy men greater honour and prestige.

The prophets tried to call the people back to the true worship of Yahweh by pleading with them to live for the future as one loving community, no longer torn apart by selfishness or greed. And for this the prophets were persecuted. They were disturbing the *status quo*, sowing subversive ideas in the minds of the common folk, encouraging the poor to make demands upon the rich and the sinful classes to criticise the religious authorities.

5

THE SUPPRESSION OF
THE MESSIAH

BY THE time of Jesus, the revolutionary ferment among a section of the People of God had reached fever-pitch, and particularly so in Galilee, which was seen as a hot-bed of dissent. The ordinary people, and especially the 'poor of Yahweh', those humble ones who waited on the Lord, were expecting that at any moment God would send a new revolutionary leader in the form of the Messiah.

And they were not disappointed. All through Jesus' life-time and beyond, men were rising up who claimed to be that Messiah, anointed by God as Christs and sent to liberate his people. Often they would take their followers out into the desert, in imitation of the wanderings of their forefathers in the wilderness. There, in that no-man's land outside Roman control, they would lay their plans for armed revolt. Then as now, the desert provided an ideal training ground for guerrilla warfare and commando tactics.

We can in fact detect, woven into the Matthew account of the destruction of Jerusalem, what may well have been an original warning given by Jesus to his own disciples against their joining such groups.

'If anyone says to you, then, "Look, here is the Christ" or "He is there" do not believe it; for false Christs and false prophets will arise and produce great signs and portents. . . . If, then, they say to you, "Look, he is in the desert," do not go there; "Look, he is in some hiding place," do not believe it' (24:23, 26).

John the Baptist seems to have been deeply involved in this general movement towards revolution. He preached the Word of God as a Word of conversion and renewal. Men had to turn

over a new leaf, bury their old way of living in the waters of the
Jordan as their ancestors had buried their lives of slavery in the
Red Sea, so as to start living for one another as their ancestors had
begun to do in the desert. For there was no time to lose – the
kingdom was on its way, round the corner, almost here.

Yet John was not the Messiah. Indeed, he was always on the
look-out for the genuine Christ. That is why he sent his disciples
to question Jesus and make sure. And Jesus himself identifies John
as the last of the prophets and the greatest – as a reincarnation,
as it were, of the prophet Elijah who was to return to earth,
according to Jewish legend, when the Messiah was about to
arrive and the revolution start in earnest. John was also, said
Jesus, the herald sent to announce the creation of a new People of
God who were to follow the Messiah out of the wreckage that
the old People of God had made of the very idea of God's kingdom and on into a glorious passover journey to the true and
everlasting kingdom.

The air round John, as he preached, must have throbbed with
the expectation of violence. As Jesus said, 'Since John the Baptist
came, up to the present time, the kingdom of heaven has been
subjected to violence and the violent are taking it by storm'
(Matt. 11:12). Not only did John call down persecution and
finally martyrdom upon himself by his words, but his message
must also have greatly encouraged parties like that of the zealots
to take up the sword for the sake of the kingdom.

The zealots saw violence as the only answer to the oppression
being suffered by the ordinary folk of Palestine, an oppression
that made nonsense of the claim that the Jews were really ruled
over by God. Though the Roman occupying force was ultimately held responsible for this, the main target for the zealots'
attack lay elsewhere.

First, they felt, the people had to be freed from the tyranny of
their own political and religious leaders, from the grip of the
priests and princelings.

The whole temple establishment, with its taxes and its laws,
tended to crush the ordinary folk and make them feel worthless

in the sight of God. For they were told that, to be really righteous, they must imitate men like the Pharisees and keep in all their detail the many rules and regulations that the scribes and the lawyers had tacked on to the rudimentary 'law of Moses'. To break any of these was to become automatically a sinner; to break the more serious ones was to become an outcast and a derelict.

Yet only men with intelligent if tortuous minds could even detect where many of these sins lay, and only men with plenty of time and money could afford to avoid them, since they lay littering every man's path so thickly that people with a living to earn or a house to run had neither the leisure nor the means to step carefully over them all. As a class, they were therefore condemned by the religious, and especially by the Pharisees, as sinners.

On the other hand, the very people who were thus despised by their clergy were also battened upon by their native aristocracy. For the rich, while looking down upon the poor, did nothing to relieve their poverty, but only helped to make them poorer.

Yet both sides of the Jewish establishment were backed up and preserved in their positions by the Romans.

It was in any case part of their invasion policy to uphold the religions of the nations they conquered, and they had gone to even greater lengths to protect the Jewish faith, since so nationalistic and exclusive a creed could only be tampered with at peril. Even Pilate, though clumsily treading on the toes of his subjects at times by offending their religious susceptibilities, was generally careful to avoid any unrest and quick to crush any disturbances, especially in the temple. That is why his headquarters overlooked the temple courts – so that he could keep an eye on things and send in the riot troops if there was any trouble, a situation that quite often arose, especially at the times of the great feasts.

Again, Pilate supported the local princes with their courts and their 'society' in much the same way that the British in the days of the raj backed up the Indian princes and the caste system. The Jewish aristocracy had little real power, however, save that of growing rich by taxing and exploiting their fellow countrymen.

But they were good for stability, since, so long as they remained in their mansions and palaces and collaborated with their over-lords, the foreignness of the Roman occupation was somewhat hidden from view and patriotic objections to it to that extent stifled.

When Jesus started preaching that the kingdom was coming at any moment; when he, too, singled out the rich, the high priests, the scribes and the Pharisees for his attacks; then the zealots must have thought that here, too, was yet another Galilaean claiming to be the Messiah and trying once again to spark off an uprising. We know that one at least of that party joined him, presumably convinced that he was to lead a violent revolution – Simon the zealot. Oscar Cullmann would go further, and say that the 'sons of thunder', James and John, who wanted to call down fire from heaven upon Jesus' opponents, were also probably zealots, and perhaps Judas Iscariot as well. Disillusionment at Jesus forbidding his followers to fight might well explain, in this case, Judas' treachery.

Cullmann claims, too, that Barabbas and the two thieves cruci-fied with Jesus were in fact rebels and violent revolutionaries. For the Romans did not normally crucify thieves. Like hanging, drawing and quartering, this was a terrible punishment reserved for the more terrible crimes, like treason and subversion. Barabbas, too, is only called brigand or robber through a mistranslation. Rebel would be the nearer word.

For the fate of rebels was the cross. Indeed, every attempt at revolution during the Roman occupation, including that of Jesus, met with suppression and, for the ring-leaders and if they were taken alive, crucifixion. In fact, when the final revolution that was to bring about the destruction of Jerusalem in A.D. 70 had been crushed, Josephus tells us that there was not enough wood to make all the crosses needed for the execution of the revolutionaries. And, at the head of the cross, a statement of the rebel's claim, the reason for his revolt, would be pinned up.

We can now understand Pilate's predicament when Jesus was brought before him and the demand made for his crucifixion.

For this man was no violent guerrilla leader, but a religious teacher with an idealistic and impossible message that men should live together as brothers. And he backed up his teaching that the kingdom of God consisted in the fellowship of man, not by force, but by the example of his own love – a love he held out even to those who were hounding him down and seeking his life, a love that sought to absorb the violence of his enemies without offering violence in return, a love that spent rather than defended itself.

Pilate was all for setting Jesus free. But, because he was afraid to upset the religious establishment of Jewry, he tried to make use of the custom of releasing a prisoner at paschal time to achieve this. In holding out before the high priests and their party the alternatives – Jesus, the non-violent visionary, and Barabbas, who would slit all their throats given half a chance – he must surely have expected their common-sense to have led them to choose Jesus.

But the shout was raised for Barabbas' release and Jesus' crucifixion. For the clergy saw more clearly than Pilate the subversive nature of Jesus' message. The revolution that he was preaching was far more dangerous, since more threatening to their position and their religion and also much more difficult to suppress, than the more open and easily-dealt-with rebellions of the zealots.

For Jesus, instead of teaching men that they could best please God by sticking rigidly to the law and worshipping regularly in the temple, showed scant regard for religious rulings and foretold a time when temple-worship would come to an end. Instead, he held that men could best worship the Father and do his will by loving one another. He said that the lists of sacred laws and the round of temple services were only useful and worthwhile if they encouraged the development of love between all the classes of what was supposed to be God's People. He dared to belittle dreadful crimes like adultery and to declare that sinners could be closer to God than men like the scribes or Pharisees.

He went further than that. He claimed that he had actually come to *replace* the temple; that he was God's special Son in whom all men, not merely Jews, could meet the Father; and, by implication, that there was no longer any need for high-priest or sacrifice.

What he was really asking for was nothing less than an abrupt and utter change in religion, a change in which the clergy would find themselves out of a job unless they fell in with his new ideas. Not that he condemned the past. On the contrary, he said that the law and the prophets were not discarded but fulfilled by him. But the religious institutions of Judaism, though they had once had their value, were apparently now outdated, even harmful, and due for transformation.

The same held good for the institutions of Jewish society. Kingly rule and noble blood had once been at the service of Yahweh and his people. But this was no longer so, and now the puppet rulers and wealthy upper classes were being asked in their turn to change their whole way of living and start being kind, fair and brotherly to the beggars at their gates. If Jesus had his way, the rich as a privileged class would disappear in one great social upheaval. And neither high priest nor Pharisee, prince nor powerful magnate wanted such a change. So they cried out for his death.

When Jesus was finally silenced on the cross and his non-violent revolution apparently crushed, it must have simply seemed that yet another self-styled Messiah had been wiped out. Though, later, the disciples were to remember in Jesus' sayings hints that neither he nor his movement would be finished off by his execution, at the present moment they could have had no reason for expecting any kind of resurgence of their leader or his message. So many Christs had already been killed without any reports of their having risen from their graves, however much their followers might have wished for it. Why should Jesus' case be any different?

Yet Jesus' followers very soon became convinced that he was still alive – indeed, was closer to them than ever before – and not just as a memory or in his ideals, but as the real and complete human being they had known in Galilee. For they had met him, in an encounter that was mysterious and strange, but nevertheless absolutely reassuring.

It was an experience they found it hard to put into words, because the Jesus they had met with had himself undergone so thorough and sudden a change that it could best be described as revolutionary in itself. He had been transformed from the lifeless corpse they had laid in the tomb, a slave to death, and from the man like themselves they had walked with on earth, a slave to human limitations, to become the man of heaven, freed for ever from every kind of enslavement.

Furthermore, he let his followers know that this was to be the outcome for everybody of the revolution he had been preaching. If human beings would only join with him in loving and serving God as their Father by giving themselves wholeheartedly to their brothers, they too would come to share in the unlimited freedom and fellowship of his glorious condition.

And so the revolution experienced by Jesus in his Easter uprising as Christ and Lord becomes in its turn the revolution of Pentecost, when his disciples, renewed in their faith in him and his message, set out to renew the hopes of the world by their preaching of that gospel. From that day to this, the Christian Church has been dedicated to the proclamation of the self-same revolutionary word.

6

THE MESSAGE OF SUBVERSION

IN ITS early days, the Church was so true to its task of preaching the Christian revolution that it found itself being ruthlessly and consistently persecuted. For it was seen as a dangerous and subversive organisation, an underground Jewish sect that threatened to undermine all authority in the Roman empire and to turn its very economy and social system upside down.

In·the first place, Christians were atheists. Though as Jews they had been allowed to be intolerant of other gods and had not been bound to worship the emperor, yet things were becoming dangerous when they were found to be instructing their gentile converts against recognising him as a god. Not that cultivated men necessarily took the emperor's claim to divinity all that seriously themselves. But the mere formalities of emperor-worship helped bolster up the whole power structure of the empire, since all authority in the state derived eventually from him. A wholesale denial of his divinity would therefore be seen, not so much as heretical, but rather as subversive. Like the Christian condemnation of war and its denigration of soldiering, this doctrine struck at the security of the state and the ruling classes, who consequently were active in their support of the persecution of the Church when it was initiated by Nero and was continued with little intermission by his successors for almost four centuries.

At the same time, the economy would also be affected adversely if Christianity really took hold. For it was already taking root among the slaves and the lower classes, and was teaching them that, in the sight of God, they were equal with their masters. Such a message might well lead to discontent, and anything that ran the risk of upsetting the system of slavery upon which Graeco-Roman civilisation and upper-class prosperity depended was to be condemned as highly dangerous.

But Nero did far less harm to the Church than Constantine. For Jesus had said that it was inevitable that his followers should be persecuted by the powers of this world. Jerusalem had always murdered the prophets, and anyone now who preached brotherly love was bound to make enemies in a society largely motivated and upheld by prejudice, self-interest and injustice.

Things are only going well for the Church, he seemed to say, when Christians are being called upon to suffer for the Gospel's sake and to give their lives for their brethren. It is when the Church has it too easy, when she is fêted, honoured, established and apparently successful that the danger of compromise creeps in, of toning down her teaching and watering down her witness so as to suit the *status quo*.

After Constantine had adopted Christianity as the official religion of the empire in the fourth century, and when to be a Christian was the respectable and even inevitable thing to do, we can see the Church very quickly losing her revolutionary fervour. Though prophets like Francis of Assisi will arise to try and renew society in the name of Christ, the official theology of the Church will be so largely derived from Greek philosophy that it will come to understand the Gospel, not in terms of revolutionary change, but of order and degree.

This *theology of order* that has been with the Church right up into the present century was based upon the old static view of the universe. We lived in an unchanging system in which things were today exactly as God had created them in the beginning. All had their allotted place in the great design, which would have been a paradise had not man spoiled the plan by refusing to play his proper role, thus upsetting the order of things.

If we were to undo the effects of this rebellion, it would be by taking our appointed place in society and living out our part as best we could. The pope must be a good pope, the king a good king, the parson a good parson and the serf a good serf. To our medieval forebears, therefore, Christendom, or a Europe in which Christ reigned in a hierarchical society by means of his hierarchical Church, was nothing less than the kingdom of heaven already begun and eager to break through.

In this static view, obedience and the preservation of order were the great virtues, revolution or criticism of the establishment the great crimes. So strong, indeed, was the horror of disobedience that, in matters of moment like warfare or apparent injustice, the authorities were always to be given the benefit of the doubt, since they were presumed to know the rights and wrongs of the case much better than the man in the street. Though they might be misleading him, even that would generally be preferable to disturbing law and order.

It is because the theology of order lingered on in the Catholic Church longer than in the other Christian Churches that we find, even in recent years, German Catholics far more subservient to Nazism, for instance, than other Christians; or an English prelate stating on television in the sixties that authority was the greatest gift the Church had to offer to men; or countries like Spain and Italy reluctant to take on social reform and allow for conscientious objection; or Catholic clergy in South Africa often far less open in their condemnation of apartheid than their counterparts in other Churches.

Eventually, however, theology had to come to terms with the evolving world-picture presented by Darwin. Strangely enough, this hammering out of a *theology of evolution* received perhaps its greatest contributions from Cardinal Newman, in his essay on the development of doctrine, and from the Jesuit, Teilhard de Chardin, though the treatment of each by the Roman authorities should show us quite clearly that the Catholic Church as a whole was far less ready to accept such a theology than less fundamentalist Christian Churches.

Vatican II was a time of optimism. Men spoke so enthusiastically of the astounding progress of the human race as it drew more and more into fellowship and marched breast forward on its triumphant journey towards the omega-Christ that it almost seemed as if sin were slipping painlessly away and mankind getting steadily better. Such an attitude distorted de Chardin's thought, which was never so naïvely optimistic as not to recognise the possibility of man's taking a wrong turning on his march. Nevertheless, it did tend to assume, hand in hand with his technical advance, an overall progress in good and a general diminishing of evil that the events of the post-conciliar years were to belie.

Harvey Cox was, in his *The Secular City*, to reflect the confident spirit of the times just after the Council, when the technological achievements of the United States and Europe were assumed to indicate an overall improvement in the whole of mankind's condition and to point out the way the non-white races must follow.

However, the intensification of the war in Vietnam, the waves of fighting sweeping over Africa, the fact of famine and hunger on an undreamt-of scale in the world, the civil rights movement and race riots in the U.S., the assassination of President Kennedy and Martin Luther King, racism in Britain finding a voice in Enoch Powell, the barricades of Bogside and Belfast, the growing realisation of the vastness of the problem of world poverty – all these factors helped bring home to the white races of the northern hemisphere that self-congratulation about their own progress was out of order, since, far from indicating a general rise in the living standards of mankind as a whole, it merely showed that such a rise had been secured by the white 15% of the earth's population largely at the expense of the 80% who are non-white and whose standards are in fact steadily falling.

Coupled with this, the popularity of Bonhoeffer's *Papers from Prison* and the diary of Ann Frank, the impact of the Eichmann trial, the controversy aroused by Hochhuth's *The Representative* and *Soldiers* and by the Defregger affair, had a cumulative effect. They reminded us of how western man had stood by, on the whole without protest, while the appalling evils of Belsen and Auschwitz, Dresden and Hiroshima were committed in his name. And they warned us, too, that it was our plain human duty to make ourselves more aware of and sensitive to our responsibility for the wickedness that exists in the world today. Hence the growth of protest movements in the west.

Hence, too, the popularity of criticisms of western society like that of the German Herbert Marcuse, now in his seventies and living in California, whose *One Dimensional Man* has been called one of the most subversive books ever to have come out of the United States.

The thought of Marcuse is said to have been one of the great inspirations of the 'May Revolution' and the student unrest of the summer of sixty-eight. It has certainly influenced the hard core of student rebels who are out, not to ensure better jobs in the future by securing a better training now, but to overthrow what they regard as an unjust and inhuman system. For Cohn-Bendit as for Marcuse, this system is equally to be found within communism as within capitalism.

Marcuse starts off his critique by accepting Marx's concept of alienation. For him, however, the mass of men in both capitalist *and* communist societies are estranged from a daily round of work that has become meaningless, boring and pointless to them. Pope Paul VI, in an address to the International Labour Organisation given in Geneva on June 10th, 1969 (and, incidentally, liberally sprinkled with quotations from Marcuse), would seem to agree. People today, the pope says, 'fulfil tasks that have no meaning for them, which cannot suffice to give them a reason for living'.

According to Marcuse, working men have in fact let themselves become enslaved, without their realising it. They do their work, not for the good of the race, not for the benefit of the human community as a whole, not even for their own enjoyment or satisfaction, but in order to earn a wage for themselves, and make a profit and win increasing power for their employers. Again, Paul at Geneva would agree that work must have 'one sole aim: not money, not power, but the good of man. . . . In work, it is man who is first and it is for man that he works.' And not, one might add, just for *a* man.

We have become accustomed to papal condemnations of communism. Pope John was the first bishop of Rome to admit publicly that there was much good in Marx. But Paul went even further, as we have seen, when he condemned out-and-out capitalism in an encyclical ('Populorum Progressio') that contains no formal condemnation of communism at all. The pope, we feel, would be at one with the statement of Archbishop Helder Câmara of Olinda and Recife, Brazil, when, speaking in London in April 1969, he said; 'Capitalism, despite its championship of the human individual and freedom, is egotistic, selfish and cruel.' But, he went on, 'super-powers professing inspiration from Marx are as cold and egotistical as their capitalist rivals'.

Marcuse is rather more precise than this. The real men of power who gain by the inhuman drudgery of the workers are, he claims, in the west the big-business corporations, and in the U.S.S.R. the bureaucrats. These groups maintain their privileged positions by a continuous process of enslavement and suppression pursued both at home and abroad.

At home, they dupe the working classes into giving their lives over to a soul-destroying routine by rewarding them with little treats that bear no real, in-built relationship to their work – a rising standard of living, annual holidays with pay, bonuses, pension schemes and so on. They need the workers to keep on producing *and* consuming, so as to ensure that their profits will roll steadily in. For profits mean power, and power means that banker or bureaucrat or board of directors can dictate to governments and manipulate society to their own satisfaction.

Profits depend upon an ever-growing rate of production and consumption. This means that the powerful ones must make use of the mass-media to create false needs among the ordinary people. If the factories are to manufacture more and more goods for the selling, then a hearty appetite for those goods will have to be engendered in the general public, until it imagines it cannot live without luxury items like electric toothbrushes or wafer-thin mints.

And the goods thus produced must not be made to last too long. 'In-built obsolescence' will ensure that cars and washing-machines soon become outdated and fall apart, with their buyers returning to trade in the wreckage for the very latest model. So the chain is maintained of over-production, over-consumption and an excessive waste in items that are often quite unnecessary for decent human living.

Although Marcuse obviously overstates his case and turns his bureaucrats and business-men into scheming and inhuman monsters into the bargain, we cannot get away from the fact that there is something very much amiss with the way trade works and wealth is distributed in our present-day world. As the rich nations' rubbish-dumps and stockpiles of unsold butter and grain rear skywards, and as their health-farms flourish and their overweight inhabitants die off from fatty hearts, so the poor third world, which provides most of the basic raw materials for the production lines of the wealthy nations, grows rapidly poorer and poorer, with 500 million of its people insufficiently fed and 10,000 dying of starvation every day.

We may find more than a grain of truth, too, in Marcuse's obviously extreme and over-simplified contention that any criticism of this system or any action that might throw the process into question and slow down the wheels of production will be opposed, discouraged, disallowed and eventually suppressed, quite ruthlessly, if need be.

Pressures, he says, are put on politicians to serve and not inspect the system if they wish to get on, and on trade-unions to co-operate, not fight, with the pattern or be labelled as subversive. The task of the teacher is, he claims, all too frequently seen as that of fitting his charges simply for taking their place in the system without cavil or demur, whether at the production line or the computer panel, in the factory, the office or the laboratory. If the artist is allowed a little more leeway in the line of criticism than other more 'serious' professionals, it will only be so long as he reaches a minority audience or can be made to seem ridiculous, eccentric or abnormal. And, in the last resort, the might and power of the law, the police and the military stands ever ready to silence protest and uphold the system by brute force.

Certainly, there are elements in Britain that resist and strongly disapprove of any adverse comment on the system. True, any protest that resorts to violent means to put its message across will meet with a correspondingly (though often less) violent response. Again, recent events in Northern Ireland have shown that it is perfectly possible for a privileged group even within the United Kingdom to make use of the forces of law and order so as to subdue and oppress its rivals. It is equally obvious that public opinion, goaded on by a slanted press and TV coverage, is intolerant of any stoppage of work, however justified, or of any attempt to drop out of society, however harmless; the striker and the hippy can look for scant sympathy from the average British citizen.

Nevertheless – and Marcuse admitted as much on a recent visit to this country – there is a basic freedom of speech and opinion allowed for in Britain at present that makes the introduction of really radical changes in our social and economic system as possible now as it was, say, in the time of the Attlee administration at the end of the last war, without either side resorting to violence, but simply through the work of influencing, educating and preparing public attitudes.

Marcuse's accusations of repression are perhaps more applicable to the United States, to Spain or to Brazil. However, he goes on to claim that, no matter how liberal and tolerant they might appear to be at home, the wealthy nations all become openly oppressive in their dealings with the under-developed or developing world. He would cite incidents like the Bay of Pigs, the Vietnam war or the Russian invasion of Prague as examples of the super-powers using naked force abroad in order, ultimately, to protect their own economic and trading interests.

For, he would hold, the developed countries of the northern hemisphere, whether communist or capitalist, depend for their growing production, consumption and wastage of the good

things of this earth, for the rise in living standards this produces
for their peoples, and for the power it gives to corporations or to
bureaucrats, upon their being able freely to continue with their
exploitation of the southern half of the globe. Any threat to the
smooth running of this procedure will consequently tend to be
met with by counter-threats of varying intensity, from the
diplomatic note to outright warfare.

While rejecting Marcuse's claim that the oppression of the
poor by the rich countries of the world is invariably a conscious
and cold-blooded piece of black-hearted devilment, or indeed
that trading interests are the predominant motive for all our
actions abroad, there are still many less radical economists,
politicians and Christians generally who would agree that there
is something terribly awry with a system that helps to reduce,
however unwittingly, the majority of men on this planet to
increasingly sub-human living conditions.

As the system stands at present, manufacturers will buy, at the
lowest possible price, what is often the single saleable commodity,
the one crop or mineral, of a poor country desperate to sell, in
order to make up what they have bought into some more
sophisticated and expensive item to be sold to their own fellow-
countrymen or their rich white neighbours. Meanwhile, the poor
country is prevented from industrialising, from building factories
to exploit its own (often abundant) raw materials. It cannot afford
the plant, which is made by the rich world at a prohibitive and
ever-increasing price. Or pressure will often be brought to bear
so as to prevent it from producing a rival to the more expensive
product of the rich country. Thus Brazil is not allowed to make
instant coffee from its own surplus crop by the United States,
whose own Maxwell House is sold round the globe.

As for aid, this is at present hopelessly inadequate, and is usually
given in the form of loans, with strings attached that demand,
first, that the money be spent with the donating country, no
matter how uncompetitive its prices, and, second, that the
borrower remain politically 'safe', and as far removed from the
idea of nationalisation as possible. Finally, the loan itself can only

be paid back by the poor country taking on further loans, since rising prices in the donor-country mean that the money it has loaned is declining in value and able to buy less and less. Far from helping the borrower industrialise, set up industry and enter the trading market of the world, it merely keeps the wolf from the door for a time. In fact, the United Kingdom is said to make an overall profit on every penny it 'gives' as overseas aid!

Furthermore, the whole system of world trade is manipulated by the developed countries to their own advantage. Trade agreements cut down import duties among the rich, thus making it even more difficult for the poor to export manufactured goods at competitive prices into the developed first world. The international monetary system, too, is the invention of the rich countries to be juggled with for their own benefit. The myth of money enables them to measure and cope with their powers of production, but works almost entirely to the disadvantage of the third world. Devaluation, for instance, not only cut the value of British aid to the underdeveloped countries suddenly and drastically, but also helped Britain to a larger share of the world market, thus leaving less room than ever for developing countries to break in.

Yet without its own industries, without its own share of world trade, the third world is powerless and can do nothing at all to improve its standards of living or to halt its steady decline into greater poverty and hunger.

Marx, says Marcuse, is unable to provide an answer to this problem. His solution to mankind's economic ills, worker-control of the means of production, is too narrow, too confined within a particular country's internal affairs, too much set in the old workers-versus-bosses mould of the nineteenth century.

The wider, world view requires, not just a change of ownership in industry, but a new way of looking at industry itself. It demands, he says, a process of 'pacification', whereby the resources of this world are used, not for the profit of the few to the disadvantage of the many, but for the good of the whole race and according to the race's real needs. And this demands the radical reorganisation of the first world's industrial, trading and money systems.

Again, Pope Paul would agree. 'The recent Council,' he tells us in 'Populorum Progressio', 'reminded us of this: "God intended the earth and all it contains for the use of all men and peoples, so created goods should flow fairly to all, regulated by justice and accompanied by charity." All other rights whatsoever, *including those of property and of free commerce*, are to be subordinated to this principle. They should not hinder but, on the contrary, favour its application. *It is a grave and urgent social duty to redirect them to their primary purpose*' (my italics).

How is this revolutionary change to be brought about? For Marcuse, it would only be sparked off by those who had not been bought by the system—by the students, the blacks and the permanently unemployed. He has since come to modify this view, which has in any case the disadvantage of not telling the students, the blacks or the unemployable what to do to create a more just society. But Marcuse is, of course, talking of *violent* revolution, and movements of this kind, he rightly says, are wholly destructive to begin with. It is only afterwards that the reshaping of society begins, not according to some detailed and pre-conceived plan, but by trial and error, by groping with difficulty after some prophetic vision. Yet the violence he advocates will fail to catch on if the aims are too sweepingly negative but only vaguely positive. The revolution will fizzle out, as it did at the Paris barricades in 1968.

Other revolutionaries, particularly in South America, have adopted guerrilla warfare as the best way to overthrow an unjust regime. We have the example of Fidel Castro's successful uprising in Cuba and the heroism of those 'martyrs of the revolution', Ché Guevara and the priest Camillo Torres, both shot as guerrilla leaders, and Régis Debray, imprisoned for his book on guerrilla warfare, 'The Revolution in the Revolution'.

Though Vatican II called for a greater awareness of the sufferings of the underdeveloped nations, it issued no invitation to armed revolt. Yet its whole message was revolutionary in the sense that it canonised and christened the very watchwords of the French revolution of 1789 – liberty, equality and fraternity. It recognised that 'the ferment of the gospel' urges men on to make freedom and brotherhood a reality. And to do so will involve radical change.

As Paul VI says, the development of human brotherhood 'demands bold transformations, innovations that go deep. Urgent reforms should be undertaken without delay'. But a change for the betterment of the human condition, and one that is both swift and deep, is precisely what we mean by revolution. Yet how is it to be accomplished? What is the Christian answer?

7

THE DEDICATION TO CHANGE

THOUGH THE need for a speedy and radical renewal of our personal attitudes and of the structures of our society in order to achieve justice for the under-privileged and non-white third world has been noted by the Churches in general as demanded by the gospel, still the individual Christian may rightly ask, 'But what can I personally do about it?'

It is to provide some kind of answer to this question that pressure-groups and protest-movements have begun to arise from within the Christian community itself. In this country, their demands begin with the modest and by now well-known request, first voiced by the Haslemere Group, that the British government donate at least 1% of the gross national product to overseas aid. Christian Aid has since adopted the same target, and Cardinal Heenan, on behalf of the Roman Catholic bishops of England and Wales, has endorsed that request, asking Catholic families and parishes to give a lead by donating 1% of their own income to the same cause.

But organisations like the Haslemere Group and the New Abolitionists go further than this. They suggest practical ways in which the world's trading and monetary systems could be changed so as no longer to favour the first world to the enormous disadvantage of the third, and ways in which Christians could witness here and now to the necessity for such a change by making specific proposals to their political leaders (see appendix).

Has Christianity anything else to add to the revolution, however, apart from its witness to the ideal of non-violence? Martin Luther King, in the well-known speech he made just a few days

before his death, likened his position to that of Moses who, having
led his people across the desert to freedom, climbed the mountain
to look over Jordan into the Promised Land, but died without
ever reaching Palestine himself. King knew that his own life was
in danger, yet he no longer felt afraid of death, for 'I have climbed
the mountain', he declared, 'I have seen the Promised Land.'

In what was almost his last speech, therefore, Martin Luther
King gave the world a message of hope. However unpromising
things might appear, he was confident that one day black
Americans and white would live together on equal terms, as
brothers.

It is this firm hope for the future that the gospel of Christ has
to add to the revolutionary movement. Despite all appearances
to the contrary, our belief in the risen Lord assures us that the
kingdom will certainly come, that human brotherhood will be
achieved, that the material advance of the white, wealthy minority
at the expense of the poor, non-white majority of men will come
to an end eventually.

Just as the Christian message gives its believers this sure hope,
so the example of Christians is meant to inject hope into the whole
movement towards human progress and brotherhood. For the
revolution is constantly under pressure to abandon hope, and that
in two ways.

First of all, it very often starts off with a burst of almost
exaggerated confidence. When organisations like 'Oxfam' or the
'War on Want' or the 'Civil Rights Movement' in the U.S. first
sprang up, people thought that here, at last, was the solution to
racism, hunger and poverty. But then, as the enormous size of
the problem revealed itself, confidence tended to give way to
despair.

The job suddenly seems far too big for any voluntary organisation. All these are doing is to scratch the surface of the problem –
give a little first-aid, keep the dying alive a little longer or tidy
up the ghetto a bit. The real and lasting solution lies with the
governments of the rich world; but they seem so preoccupied
with raising their white voters' standards of living and fiddling

about with their own internal problems that any grant of useful aid to the third world or of genuine equality to black Americans seems out of the question.

The witness of Christians when faced with these attitudes is to testify that man is not alone in his task; that his efforts at evolving into one single community are ways in which he co-operates with the creative work of God; that the love a man tries to show his fellows is his partaking of the Spirit of Jesus, in whom all are being drawn into unity; and that, eventually, the community of the future, the communion of saints, will certainly arrive – but not until the end of history.

We should not be so presumptuous, then, as to think that we can create the kingdom on our own or in our lifetime. For, when we find that we can't, we will be inclined to give up in despair. Instead, we must have the hope to work for the fulness of brotherhood that is certainly to come as the result of our struggles, and despite any successes that might delude us into thinking that we have already arrived at the Promised Land, or any failures that might make us feel that we have set ourselves an impossible target.

For it is man's constant temptation to resist change. He wants to see himself succeed and settle down securely to a pattern of life that he can predict and control and fully understand. And this is true of the Left as well as of the Right. The conservative suspects change as generally bad, and will only reluctantly allow for reforms. Socialism, too, tends to get stuck in one period of history, as, for example, Russian Communism or the British Labour movement, and re-live the old battles from the days of its glory rather than going on to fight new ones. Its ideas become fixed, its principles inflexible, its institutions fossilised.

If the Church, as we have said, represents the true condition of the human race as, in fact, under grace and destined for glory, then she, too, must reflect and encourage this human necessity for change in her very structures and life.

By her own readiness to adapt herself – her organisation, her preaching, her worship – to the changing needs of the world, she must show that she is not, in fact, established or settled down on this earth, wedded neither to one particular culture or historical period or spot on the surface of the globe. She must appear as truly catholic, truly representative of all mankind and not as a religious organisation that is dominated by white interests, by the outlook of the wealthy industrialist and by the yearning to turn back the clock to the days of her political dominion in Europe. Instead, she is meant to present herself as a poor pilgrim community, the People of God on its way to the Promised Land.

Thus she will be making clear and acknowledging before God, on behalf of the whole human race, what is really going on in mankind's struggle for brotherhood. For, in fact, the whole of the human race, in so far as it concerns itself with creating community, is this People of God, and the brotherhood it seeks to achieve is the true goal of its pilgrimage, the kingdom of heaven. And this means that the race can never settle down as though that goal had been reached, but must be dedicated to the idea of change, constantly prepared to scrap ideas or institutions that get in the way of this target instead of helping towards it.

Mao's principle of 'perpetual revolution' is in this sense perfectly true. For if, as Pope Paul said in Geneva, 'Brotherly love is the only *lasting* cement with which to build up the city of man', then Church and world must be always on the look-out to ensure that nothing in either society is impeding the growth of this brotherly love.

And this means constant change. For, like Pharisaism, even the best institutions of men soon become obsolete and obstructive when the situation that called them into being no longer exists. One need only think of the need for trade union reform in this country or for the reform of the Roman curia that was called for by Vatican II, to see how easily this can happen in Church and state.

To resist change on principle is therefore anti-Christian. And this needs to be said, since the growing right-wing backlash that we see at work in the western world is also being felt in the western Church. The attempt to tone down the Vatican Council's teachings and to dilute its spirit, backed up by a frantic appeal to the way in which the present pope often expresses his justifiable fear of change merely for change's sake, is frequently accompanied by the application of abuse, heresy charges and all kinds of pressure to those who hold a more open, biblical and conciliar view of Christianity.

Not that the two attitudes are confined to the Roman Church, for they are to be found in all the major Christian denominations so that the progressive Catholic, though verbally in agreement with his conservative co-religionist, may well find he has much more in common as regards his overall understanding of Christianity with a progressive Methodist or Baptist. In their sense of what is important about the Christian message and what is the main purpose of Christian living, the conservative and progressive are poles apart.

But, as Professor Metz has recently pointed out, the radical progressive is generally too humane to return the charges of heresy and the attempts to drive him out of their own version of the Church that are made by his conservative fellow-believers. Instead, he may attempt to maintain a dialogue with his detractors and generally will hide from them the depth of his disagreement. Yet, says Metz, surely he has a duty to witness to the gospel by stating plainly, but charitably, not that there is room for either view within the Church, but that the conservative position is frankly not Christian.

For conservatism in religion seeks a false security in rules and formulæ and ways of worship that seem to be unchanging and unchangeable. These reassure him in his personal, individual quest for salvation, which he sees as a piece of private enterprise or of self-fulfilment in which, to be sure, he may make use of his poor neighbour by performing acts of charity towards him, since these help on the quest of personal sanctification enormously. The world may thus be exploited as a rich means of grace, but it is otherwise rejected as meaningless so far as religion is concerned.

This faithfully echoes extreme political conservatism (though not necessarily the Conservative), which sees man's life as a struggle for self-fulfilment in a stable social set-up in which he can predict where his profit lies. It seeks a false security in an unchanging and permanent establishment, in the superiority of a particular race or country or way of life or class, and it makes use of the world as the means for strengthening and increasing that security by bolstering up the establishment more and more.

If the Church of Christ reflects this conservative attitude, she should only do so by showing how it is at variance with all idea of human brotherhood and is, in consequence, profoundly anti-Christian. For Jesus came, not to bring security to a privileged minority of the human race, but to bring a sword. He came to cast on the earth the fire of his challenge, the challenge for human beings to love one another as he has loved them.

The Church is meant to witness to the need for the non-violent revolution that this challenge entails, the revolution towards brotherhood and equality between rich and poor, black and white, male and female. And she should do so by allowing the revolution to take place in her own ranks. She is bearing false witness when she appears to be preoccupied with financial matters, dominated by white interests, on the side of the wealthy and powerful, and reflecting officially a purely masculine point of view.

Above all, the Church needs prophets. And in this she again reflects a need of the world. For the world, and especially the west, needs leaders and politicians who can really speak to the people, particularly to the young. If young people are disenchanted with democracy and the party system, it is because that system seems able blithely to ignore what they would consider to be the crying needs of the day. In Britain, the Labour Party seems so preoccupied with the memory of the hungry thirties and so relieved to find that many workers are now quite well-off that it will do anything the international bankers ask to preserve and increase the standard of living. The Tories, on the other hand, seem set on restoring power and prestige to our little island, and especially to its upper classes, and are lost in reveries of empire and the golden days when one had servants. Though paying lip-service to the notion of black equality, the rank and file of the party are suspected of sympathising with Ian Smith and with Enoch Powell in their hearts.

Young people today are full of enthusiasm for human rights and of genuine concern for the underprivileged and the suffering, as anyone who has worked among them will know. What they want to hear, instead of the selfish, worn-out words of too many of the politicians, are the words of a prophet who will speak to them in terms of their country's duty towards the whole human family, and of ways of carrying it out.

Similarly, the Church needs prophetic leadership. She needs theologians who can say something to the ordinary people, and not just to one another; who can leave to one side the long-dead squabbles and the problems they have created among themselves in order to talk to us about the revolution and what it means in terms of the gospel; who can show us how what is happening in the world relates to our Christian beliefs, and how a fuller understanding of Jesus' words will help us better co-operate with all generous-hearted men in the continual process of changing the world until it arrives at the glory of the risen Christ.

Likewise, we need prophetic leadership among our clergy. Men who seem primarily interested in keeping the old institutions going, no matter how obsolete; who insist that the apathy of the people towards sermons and missions that are out-of-date comes from lack of faith and not a Christian instinct for the worthless and misleading; who seem satisfied to spend their days doing little routine jobs that often seem pointless to outsiders and bear little relevance to the gospel; who betray a deep fear of any kind of change, even in the kind of clothing a clergyman should wear; who make pursuits like liturgical reform or ecumenism seem much more important than the task of loving one's neighbour; such people fail to give any lead or inspiration to the young, far less to convince them that the clerical vocation is really worth while or self-sacrificing in any useful way. To join

the V.S.O. can seem far more of a Christian vocation than entering a seminary or a convent.

Though not professing to be a theologian; though a pastoral
bishop for only a short time in his career; though shaped by his
long years in the diplomatic service of the Vatican; though
temperamentally inclined more to depression than to cheer-
fulness; nevertheless, Paul VI has himself raised a prophetic
voice with regard to the greatest problem of our age and the
greatest test presented to us as Christians today. In so doing, he
has shown that to be revolutionary in spirit is not just a matter of
temperament or choice. He has also reminded us that the temptation either stubbornly to oppose all change or to accept too readily
and violently any kind of change at all must be resisted equally
if we are to remain true to the genuine and continual revolution
demanded by the gospel teaching on brotherly love.

The pope summed up the urgency of this task in article 29 of
'Populorum Progressio' when he said:

'We must *make haste*, as too many are suffering, and the distance
is growing that separates the progress of some and the stagnation,
not to say the regression, of others.'

8

THE DE-RITUALISATION
OF WORSHIP

The Sacramental Situations

WE HAVE seen how, in Jesus and on our behalf, a human being hears the Word of God so fully as to *be* that Word made flesh, and responds to that Word so completely as to *be* the Son of God in human form. We have seen how the Church, in her turn the representative and stand-in for all mankind, openly acknowledges Jesus as that Word, and in so doing gives herself explicitly, with him, to the Father in reply.

The Church therefore expresses, as far as it has been revealed, the true reality of the human condition. Men are always being challenged, in fact, by God's Word to give themselves to him by dedicating themselves to the good of the race. They are being continually called to the revolution, at once personal and social, implied in the concept of brotherly love.

But God only saves men by revealing himself to them. Thus, at any period in the race's history, there must be representatives of that race who will hear and openly recognise the Word of God as explicitly as it is being uttered, so that the fulness of salvation might be available, at that particular point in time, to the whole human community. Jesus saves us by standing in for us and accepting God's revelation of himself on our behalf. And, since Jesus has left our earth, the Christian community goes on acknowledging, in him, the Father's saving Word made flesh, as representing the larger community of man at this particular moment in its history. And, in recognising the underlying Christian reality behind the human condition, the believing Church co-operates with the creative Word of God in making that reality a fact.

But it is not just Jesus' *condition* that the human race shares and the Church expresses. Though it is always his condition to be Son and Word of the Father, this personal vocation into which he was born has to be lived out in all the varying situations of his earthly life until it reaches its fulness in his rising from the dead. Every *situation*, then, was a time for Jesus to hear the Word calling him to express his sonship by a particular form of loving service towards both God and man. On our behalf, then, and in all the events of his earthly existence, Jesus was open to his Father's will, as Word, and responsive to it, as Son, as fully as might be until that open-ness, that responsiveness reached its perfection in his death and resurrection.

The same holds true for mankind in general. By the common humanity we all share with Jesus, each one of us is called to share his condition to the full. But this call we receive at our own entry into the race must be lived out personally in all the events of our daily lives until we, too, have risen with Christ to glory. In every human situation, we are called to hear the Word of God, who is Jesus, inviting us to give ourselves with him as sons to the Father by offering ourselves to our brethren in some particular form of service.

Not that we will necessarily be conscious of this fact. The degree of our awareness of the encounter with God that is to be made in the situations of our everyday lives will vary according to the fulness (or otherwise) of our explicit belief in Jesus. But the degree to which we actually respond to the Word that lies behind the situation by the giving of ourselves, in him, to God will depend, not upon whether we recognise this encounter for what it is, but upon the way in which we put into practice the demand for brotherly love that it makes upon us.

The Christian explanation of what is really happening to us in our day-do-day human situations is set out most clearly in the sacraments of the Church. These activities of the Christian community express and refer back to the activity of Christ himself in his hearing and responding to his Father's call in all the events of his own earthly life. They are meant to express, too, the fact that all human beings, and not only Christians, are able to share in that response of Christ in all the circumstances of their own daily lives. And they point to the fact that there will come a time when we will no longer hear and respond to the Word of God partially in daily event or Christian sacrament, but when our response shall be total in our rising from the dead.

The sacraments are not to be seen as means of grace or sources of the Spirit in the sense that, by their performance, they win for their participants some superior kind of life-force, some spiritual advantage not available to other men. Rather, they are means of grace to the Christian because they best express and celebrate a reality that is already taking place, not only in his own life, but in the lives of his fellow human-beings.

For the believer, then, the sacrament will either represent the completion of an encounter with the Word that has already begun in his ordinary daily living, or it will be a worthless piece of ceremonial as far as he is concerned. The human events and situations in which he finds himself involved will contain for him an invitation to go on and celebrate their true meaning more fully and explicitly in the sacraments. Thus he will be called to take his place in a community that recognises, in its worship and on behalf of the whole community of man, the Word of God that lies behind human affairs.

Though we may say that the sacraments will not be necessary for the salvation of the majority of men, inasmuch as they can meet God just as fully in the situations of each day, yet they *will* be necessary for the Christian, and that in two ways.

First, because he is called thus to express to the full what is going on in the world, so that to refuse that invitation would be, for him, a rejection of God's presence in all human encounters. And second, because, by his taking his place in the Church at worship, he helps it act as stand-in for the race at large and recognise, on mankind's behalf, the full Christian reality that underlies its life.

And this representative function *is* necessary for the salvation of all men. Without it, ordinary human events and situations at this moment in history would lose the very value and meaning to which the sacraments bear witness. For, if God saves us *all* by revealing himself to *some*, then we may all meet with that salvation of his in our daily experiences as human beings because his revelation of that fact is accepted explicitly by the Christian Church in her sacramental worship.

Indeed, the sacraments themselves are representative of a whole range of human activities in which man may encounter the saving Word of God. They take up and celebrate certain basic situations in such a way that their religious dimension is made plain to the worshippers.

Or so it should be. For the sacraments ought not to seem like magical rites aimed at putting the privileged few in touch with an otherwise-absent deity, or like mysterious and arcane ceremonies that bring God within the grasp of a minority group to its own exclusive advantage. Though, as celebrations of a community, they must needs submit to a certain amount of ordering and formalisation, they should never be allowed to become so swamped by ritual as to lose their vital connection with the situations of normal, everyday life. After all, it is precisely in their expressing the hidden value of ordinary human living that they help to save and redeem mankind.

Baptism

The sacrament of baptism expresses the Christian reality that lies behind every human being's initiation into the race. It celebrates the normal situation where a member of that race first begins to love other people in a fully human way, leaving behind him a childish and self-centred style of living in order to give himself, as an adult, to his own community.

This initiation into the family of man is, in fact, an individual's entry, as a complete human being, into communion with his God. For the love that binds one person to another is in fact the Spirit of the risen Lord that binds him, at the same time, to Christ and, through him, to his Father. Thus, a man's entry into the human race is, in all reality, his entry into the People of God and a time when he begins to play his part in drawing the whole race into one fellowship in the Spirit and so helps bring about the kingdom that is coming.

The Christian reality of this situation is expressed by a ritual plunge into, and a rising out of, a pool of water. This action represents that plunge into the grave with Jesus, and that rising with him from the slavery of sin to a share in the new life of the Spirit, that always takes place whenever human beings start to love one another. It expresses the re-creation and re-birth in that Spirit that all men experience as soon as they learn to forsake the enclosed world of their childhood and begin to live for other people. Thus the entry into the Church community that is brought about by baptism stands for this entry into the larger community of mankind that human beings achieve as they approach adult status.

The greatest barrier, it seems to me, to a more meaningful celebration of this sacrament lies in our present-day practice of baptising babies. The usual procedure in the early Church and for the first four hundred years of its existence was to treat baptism as a sacrament primarily for adults and coming as the full expression of a grown-up human-being's decision to become a Christian. For him, such an expression was necessary to complete the decision he had already in some way arrived at, the decision that he must try and live for other people.

Infant baptism seems only to have become the regular practice as a result of theologians interpreting too rigorously and legalistically Jesus' command that men hear the gospel and receive baptism. Our Lord is obviously talking, first of all, about adults and not about children. Secondly, he is condemning only those adults who, having really heard and believed in the gospel, still refuse to be baptised. For them, this is indeed to reject Jesus Christ himself and the salvation that he came to bring.

For those who, through no fault of their own, do not believe, and above all, therefore, for those who, like infants, are incapable of making an act of faith at all, this saying of Jesus obviously cannot apply. The fact that it was thought to do so and the opinion that the most any unbaptised baby could hope for in the afterlife was the 'natural happiness' of a 'limbo' set apart from the life of heaven led to the wholesale administration of the sacrament to the children of Christian parents, with the consequence that the rite is often treated as little more than magic.

Infant baptism really means, however, not that this particular baby has some advantage over his unbaptised brothers and sisters in so far as, if he dies in infancy, he will go to heaven and they to limbo, but that all human beings are born into a sinful race so that, when they grow up, they must make a definite choice against sin and for God.

This choice the baptised child will come to ratify, it is hoped, in later years by deciding to try and live for others, and by recognising that, in doing so, he is dedicating himself, in the Spirit of the risen Christ, to God the Father. The unbaptised on the other hand, will make that decision without understanding the Christian reality beneath it. He will simply enter into adult human relationships with other people, try to do good to them, try to love them.

Again, infant baptism has meant that the sign of the sacrament, literally a ducking of the convert to Christianity under water, has had to be whittled down in the west to a mere pouring of a little water upon a child's forehead. So obscured has the meaning of baptism in consequence become that it has popularly been taken as, in the first place, not a plunge into the death and rising of Jesus, but simply a ritual washing-away of sin.

It seems probable that, the more the view gains ground that unbaptised babies who die in childhood are not thereby excluded from the kingdom of heaven, so a general move towards adult baptism will gradually develop. It may well be that the children of Christian parents of the future will, after perhaps being dedicated to God in their infancy, only come to the immersion of baptism by their own free and responsible choice as they grow towards adulthood. In other words, the present practice and witness of the Baptist Churches may well find wider favour.

Thus de-ritualised, the sacrament would no longer be seen simply as the way to get hold of a special kind of life that the unbaptised, as children, cannot receive at all, and only with difficulty when they grow up. Instead, baptism would be taken as a definite act of commitment to Christ – in the first place, by acknowledging and loving his presence among men, and secondly in recognising this presence explicitly and thanking God for it on behalf of the human race in the worship of the Church. It would be regarded as a real dedication to the revolution of brotherly love that conscience and the Christian gospel both demand, and hence a genuine submersion of self-interest for the good of the human family that will be a real participation in the death and resurrection of Jesus.

Confirmation

Confirmation, as the completion of Christian initiation, was originally given along with baptism as an integral part of a single rite, as indeed it still is among eastern Christians. That is because the ordinary human situation it expresses is one that goes hand in hand with a man's full entry into the human community.

Every human being who sees the need for revolution – that is, for human institutions and human hearts to be perpetually judged and, if need be, reformed in accordance with the standard of brotherly love – has the further duty of *testifying* to his belief in that need before the world. He must be a witness to the revolution if it is ever to come about.

For the revolution needs its prophets – agents of subversion who will speak out on behalf of the under-privileged and unloved, who will use their talents to put the message across with power, and who will have the courage to face the persecution that will surely follow. Every reformer has had his martyrdom, whether at the hands of police or of press or of public opinion. But he has found the strength to put up with his trials in the hope that, some day, men will live richer and fuller lives because of him.

Reformers and revolutionaries of this calibre do not generally emerge from the existing authority-structures and institutions of the world. Rather, they rise up from among the people, usually to challenge those authorities and institutions in so far as they hinder human brotherhood. That is why men like William Wilberforce or Danilo Dolci, Earl Russell or Des Wilson, were and are regarded as great nuisances, if nothing worse, by the upholders of the status quo. For they are obviously out to convert public attitudes until eventually, by their pressure, they will have changed the cherished practices of officialdom itself. This conformist reaction was illustrated with remarkable candour in a speech given by John Braine, the author and a Roman Catholic, to the Right-wing Monday Club in London on June 23rd, 1969. 'We had quite enough,' he said, talking about programmes on the B.B.C., 'about the death of Martin Luther King. We have sympathy for his widow, but he was a troublemaker and a very stupid man.'

But the witness that men like King make will be, in reality, a testimony to the Christ who commands us to show our love for his Father by loving our neighbour, and who opens out for our sharing his own relationship of love with God and the human race. It is in the power of this Spirit of love that we are, in fact, urged to speak out, often against wrongs in the institutions of Christianity as well as in the world at large, for the need for a revolution that will create a brotherhood of man that is really nothing less than the reign of Christ and the kingdom of God.

The persecution, however slight, that we will have to put up with will be our personal sharing in the passion and death of our Saviour, who died for his preaching of the gospel, while the firmer love it induces in us will be our deeper participation in his rising from the powers of evil. It will be our growth in grace.

We express the Christian reality behind this call to witness in the sacrament of confirmation. Here, a sign of commission – an anointing with oil, a laying-on of hands – represents, in fact, our being sent out into the world to testify to a message of brotherly love that is, in its fulness, the gospel of Christ, by a power that is, in reality, his Spirit.

But the problem today is, again, that the sacrament is often given at an unsuitable age. In the east, its link with baptism is maintained at the expense of obscuring its meaning, since it is hard to appreciate the commissioning of a babe-in-arms to the task of proclaiming the kingdom. In the west, it has been taken away from baptism but is still normally administered before it can fully express a genuine reality in the life of the child, and so runs the danger of being regarded as a magical or meaningless ceremony.

The solution, the necessary de-ritualisation, would seem to lie in two directions. First, one wonders whether the anointing with oil or the Jewish custom of the laying-on of hands say anything clearly and obviously to western man today. Therefore the question arises whether or not the Church could change the rite and make use of some more obvious form of commissioning and empowering.

While the answer as to how far the details of the rite have been specified by Christ and how drastically the Church could adapt them must lie in the future and in the way the rite develops in time to come, the second problem is capable of speedier solution. However long infant baptism may endure – perhaps for all time – confirmation at least could be given at an age when it can really express the Christian reality behind a person's genuine and heart-felt decision to witness to the need for brotherly love in our world, and, as a believer, to testify to the risen Lord as source and model for that love. The contrary desire to move confirmation back to unite it with infant baptism seems to me a piece of pedantry and a backward step in more ways than one. In the present situation, we must surely endure the untidiness of having the two parts of the initiation rite separated from each other as the best we can do at the moment if we are to have one of those parts celebrated at a more apt and suitable age.

The Eucharist

The eucharist, too, is meant to make plain the real meaning behind a perfectly ordinary kind of human situation. It expresses the Christian reality within what occurs when human beings meet one another in friendship and when they celebrate their fellowship together. It tells us of the underlying truth beneath all joyful and loving re-unions and of the deeper desire such encounters produce to give oneself more generously in fellowship to the other members of the group and, beyond them, to the human community as such.

In fact, this entering into communion with other people is a communion with Jesus Christ. He it is whom we meet in our neighbour, he it is whose love we are sharing in our fellowship one with another, he it is who binds us in covenant more firmly to mankind and to his heavenly Father. He feeds us, as it were, with the Spirit of love – but only in so far as we sacrifice ourselves, offer ourselves with him to our companions, to our race, and therefore to our God.

All this we express in the eucharistic meal. Here, our recognition of the body of Christ that is being built up in the human race as men draw together in loving unity leads us to feed on the body of Christ under the sign of bread. And these meetings we make with the members of our race are acknowledged here as encounters with Christ in whom we are all made one. In this sacred meal, we make plain and complete for ourselves and on behalf of the race the full Christian reality behind our everyday attempts to give ourselves to other people by showing that such self-sacrifice is, whether we know it or not, the offering of ourselves, through the Christ who is present in our neighbour, to God our Father.

The eucharist is thus a revolutionary meal. When we eat it, we claim not only to be at peace with our brothers and sisters gathered round the same table of the Lord but also with mankind in general. To eat the eucharist is to dedicate ourselves, not just to those who eat with us, but also to our brothers and sisters in the ghetto, in the slum, in the third world or in the war-torn battle-ground. It is to commit ourselves to the cause of Christ which is the brotherhood of man. We cannot, if our eating has been genuine and sincere, get up from the eucharistic table to go out and exploit or suppress or impoverish other members of our race, failing to recognise them for what they really are – members of the body of Christ we have just received.

The more that the meal aspect of the mass is itself obscured by ritual, the more this commitment can be dodged, or turned into a mere formality; the ritual meal is in danger of producing only a ritual commitment. Anything that throws the meal element into sharp and unavoidable prominence is therefore to be welcomed, whether it be through the extension of existing practices like the house-mass or communion under both kinds, or through a growing demand for the use of real bread and its reception in the hand, smaller parishes or their division into smaller eucharistic groups, or a greater informality and freedom in worship.

It is very difficult, if invited to a meal with friends, not to feel committed to them in the eating of the meal. Indeed, if one were not prepared to give oneself to one's fellows at the table, one would feel unable to accept their invitation. It should be so with the eucharist. One should feel a fraud if one were to go to mass and receive communion without any care for the rest of the people in the church, or while remaining quite unprepared for any inner revolution of the heart that might lead one to further the Christian revolution outside in the world.

The Sacrament of Penance

As for penance, this surely sums up the Christian meaning behind the reintegration of the offender back into the human community. It is meant to show that offences against that community, deeds that harm human fellowship, injustices that hinder the brotherhood of man are in fact offences against God. They are, in other words, sins.

Sins like this can only be undone by means of a personal revolution, by the turning over of a new leaf, by a conversion that will be a return to the human community from which one had to some extent isolate oneself by exploiting or abusing one's fellows.

To become aware, with regret, of the way one has failed to serve the cause of brotherhood in the past and to determine to make good the harm done by a greater effort at serving humanity in the future, will in fact be a reconciliation, not just with the community, but, through Christ, with God.

This fact is made explicit in the sacrament. Here, a man's return to God and the human family is represented by the Christian's return to the local church-community, there plainly to acknowledge his anti-social behaviour as an offence against God and men and to seek pardon from both through the representative of God and the Church, the ordained minister.

The sacrament of penance, however, will fail to express as fully as it might the Christian truth that lies behind all human works of reconciliation if it seems to be a private and non-communal affair. But a more public form of celebration will also require a more demanding attitude and a greater sensitivity towards sin. If we are to see our sins as offending God by attacking human fellowship and our return to God as a return, simultaneously, to the ideal of universal brotherhood, then we will no longer be satisfied with a routine and perfunctory confession of a list of rather trivial misdemeanours.

Rather than reciting all the ways we have broken a law of God that is seen as some definite and limited set of rules, we will want to confess how deeply inadequate has been our whole effort at conforming to the true law of Christians, Jesus Christ himself. Until we can give ourselves to our brethren as completely as he, we can never be satisfied with our performance – though, by the more easy-going standards of the rules and regulations to be found in the old-fashioned forms of examination of conscience, we may not have offended one little bit.

If a more authentic celebration of penance is to be achieved, then anything that tends to make the sacrament undisturbing and routine, and de-fuses it of its revolutionary content so that it is no longer taken as a further commitment to brotherly love, will have to be rejected. This may well mean, for some, that they find they ought to 'go to confession' less frequently, or that it tends to be more of an exceptional and memorable event in the life of the Catholic Christian.

Matrimony and Holy Orders

Again, orders and marriage, as sacraments, are meant to bring out the real meaning of certain states of life and functions in society. As the one who presides over the Christian community and directs and helps its worship, the bishop, priest or deacon is meant, not to dominate, but to serve his brethren. And his service will be to draw his community more closely together, to unify it into one fellowship in the Spirit of Christ, to make of it a truly loving family that is open to the needs, not just of its members, but of the whole world.

Just as this family which is the Church represents before God and makes explicit the true condition of the *human* family, so its ordained ministers make plain the true nature of authority among men. They show that this, too, is meant to be a service towards the community. In other words, those in positions of power are intended to use that power, not in an oppressive way and for their own advantage, but in order to help human beings grow together in a fellowship that is, in reality, the work of the Spirit of Christ.

But they must set their sights wider than their own particular communities if they are to do this, just as the clergy ought to look beyond the needs of their parish, their diocese, their Church or the Christian religion. The politician, the businessman, the banker, the bureaucrat must see further than national self-interest and prestige or company profits and expansion, and use his extensive if not always obvious powers to further the cause of the world-wide family of man.

Instead, as we have seen, all too often those in authority and the great powers of the world, however tolerant and liberal they may seem at home as they bask in the approval of a people that enjoys an ever-rising standard of living, not only exploit the world's poor abroad, but back up their depradations and defend their own interests with a vast show of naked force. Furthermore, if the injustice of such an abuse of authority and power is at all questioned, then the same naked force is liable to be used against such subversion at home.

Authority in the Church, therefore, if it is to witness to its own true Christian meaning as service of the brethren, must speak out clearly on behalf of the revolution. Pope Paul and Archbishop Câmara could be said, in this respect, to be living examples of the way our Christian leaders ought to try and reform the use of power in the world. Or the bishops of Rhodesia in their stand against the new constitution. Or Bishop Trevor Huddleston, who once contested the power of white South Africa so courageously on behalf of the black population and is now speaking out, from Stepney, on behalf of the homeless 'squatters' threatened by town-hall bureaucracy. It is heartening to read how, in defence of his position, he said in June 1969, 'What is the early Christian Church about except revolution? The early Christians were called "the men who turned the world upside down".'

Herbert McCabe's analogy between the priest and the guerrilla leader is therefore not as far-fetched as it might at first sound. Through his ministry of a Word that speaks of revolution and of sacraments that commit to revolution, he is himself meant to inspire other men to bring about the upheaval in their own lives and in society that the kingdom requires, by laying bare the injustice in their midst.

Those who resent such interference would prefer to see the priest or bishop in a ritual rather than a revolutionary role. They would prefer to keep him a man set apart, confined to church and presbytery, marked out by quaint clothing, surrounded by an aura of other-worldly piety and living up to his respectable middle-class status. It is for the clergy themselves, therefore, to reject such a role and to de-ritualise their own position if they are to appear before men with the genuine authority of the gospel of Jesus Christ.

Again, Christian marriage displays and expresses the true reality beneath all human marriage by declaring that this loving union between a man and a woman is their participation in the Holy Spirit, who unites them both to Christ as bride to groom.

Unfortunately, the present marriage laws of the Roman Catholic Church – her prohibition of a Catholic marrying in the church of the non-Catholic partner, the demand that all the children of such a marriage be reared as Roman Catholics even though this may be against the non-Catholic partner's conscience, the talk of validity and non-validity that the clergy can hardly explain or the laity understand, the scandal of the easy divorce for a Catholic who has contracted what his Church would call an invalid marriage – all these make it appear that only full Roman Catholic marriages are truly blessed.

If Christian marriage is meant to witness to the dignity and Christian value of *all* marriages, then it will be for Christians to protect and defend marriage everywhere. This will be made evident, not only by their conscientious attempts at assessing the morality of contraception, divorce or abortion, but also by their protesting at inadequate housing, insufficient wages for bringing up a family, the enforced chastity of long separations while, for instance, the husband works in the mines of Johannesburg or Bolivia, or on long stretches of shift work in the factory, and so on. To uphold marriage and the family will once more lead to revolution.

The Anointing of the Sick

The anointing of the sick, on the other hand, explains the real significance of all works of healing as aimed, not simply at restoring bodily health, but at restoring a whole and complete human being back to the community and to a renewed dedication to contribute to its fellowship. This, says the sacrament, will in fact be a cure from the sickness of sin and a fuller restoration to grace, or the Spirit of the Lord.

And so seven sacramentalised situations display the revolutionary call to universal brotherhood that is to be found in our ordinary, every-day human situations, and reveal this call as, in fact and whether men are aware of it or not, an encounter with the Word of God and a sharing in his Spirit. The Christian comes to the sacrament to express that encounter explicitly before God on behalf of his fellow men, and to find what will be for him (though not for them) its necessary fulfilment and completion.

APPENDIX

A. THE HASLEMERE PROGRAMME ...
AS REGARDS BRITAIN

'More particularly, we believe that Britain should:

'1. Increase aid by 1970 from £205 million to at least £300 million. By 1975 it should be at least £600 million and by 1980 at least £2,000 million (which is less than the present defence budget).

'2. Provide all aid to developing countries in grant form. Waive all interest and capital payments on past aid.

'3. Take the initiative in opening international discussions on the means to arrange an automatic transfer of resources.

'4. Abolish all quotas, subsidies and other trade restrictions affecting the exports of developing countries. Abolish or reduce, if necessarily unilaterally, tariffs on their exports.

'5. Work out and promote an international scheme to raise the income from primary commodities.

'6. Co-operate constructively and effectively in UNCTAD negotiations. Make sure that in any future round of GATT negotiations on trade restrictions the problems of developing countries receive priority.

'7. Do all it can to ensure that any newly created international liquidity (such as the Special Drawing Rights) will be disbursed solely to developing countries.

'8. Resist the pressure of lobbies whose interests conflict with those of developing countries. Refrain from economic retaliation and military action against poor countries which take radical political and economic initiatives of which they disapprove.'

(For further information about the Haslemere Group, including the full text of its Programme and Declaration, contact *Stephen Duckworth, 66 Cambridge Gardens, London W.10.*)

B. THE NEW ABOLITIONISTS

The New Abolitionists are a group of concerned people who try to ensure that, amidst competition for time and money, the needs of the poor countries are pressed at Westminster.

Aims and Principles

'In the long term the New Abolitionists are looking for a radical narrowing of the gap between the rich and the poor of the world. Basic to their attitude is a belief in the right of developing countries to determine their own future, their own political forms and their own social relations. They oppose attempts by developed countries to tie aid to their own political advantage or to retaliate against developing countries which take political or economic steps of which they disapprove.

'The broad aims of the group are to work for:

'1. A transfer of 1% of Britain's gross national product annually to the developing countries by 1972.

'2. Initiatives by Britain on commodity agreements for primary products which constitute the bulk of the developing world's exports.

'3. The reduction of Britain's tariff barriers where these discriminate against the manufactures of the developing countries.

'4. British support for the disbursement to the developing countries of a disproportionate amount of any newly created international liquidity.

'5. An increase in the *long-term* private investment in the developing countries.'

(For further information contact *Miss Joan Reilly*, 'New Abolitionists', *16 Alton Road, Richmond, Surrey*.)

C. THE CHURCHES' ACTION FOR WORLD DEVELOPMENT

Declaration on World Poverty

'We, the undersigned, believe that mass hunger, disease and illiteracy are intolerable anywhere in the world. The international financial and trading systems can and must be changed to obtain justice among men. The poorer countries must receive more aid, and the terms of international trade must no longer discriminate against the poor. As a first step we ask you as our representative in Parliament to support:

'1. The negotiation of trade agreements favourable to the less developed countries;

'2. Government initiatives for international monetary reform related to the needs of the less developed countries;

'3. The allocation by 1972 of at least 1% of the gross national product of Great Britain for overseas aid (with at least three-quarters of this target in the form of official government aid).

'We hereby commit ourselves to action for world development.'

(This is the text of the declaration used in the National Sign-in on World Poverty in January 1970.)

D. SAMPLE LETTER

'Britain is now giving £210 million a year. Half of this is in the form of loans. Some people think the loans are not repaid. We are, in fact, getting back £60 million every year in repayments and interest. That brings the cost down to £150 million.

'Most of our aid is used to buy British goods. This means that two-thirds of it comes back to this country and does not cost our balance of payments anything. So the £210 million costs the balance of payments only £70 million. Then we get the £60 million back – some of that would have been used for exports anyway. Taking both points together, the balance of payments cost is, say, £30 million.

'So, if Britain alone stopped *all* aid, we would only gain £30 million on the balance of payments. If all western countries stopped aid, Britain would quite certainly be worse off on the balance of payments.

'Some people complain that British aid is not used to buy the products of *their* industry. They do not realise that switching to their industry could only be done at the expense of some other British industry.

'Britain does not give more aid than most other countries. The French, with a smaller population, give more than half as much again as we do, and the Americans give more than half the world total. The percentage of our GNP given in aid has been falling steadily since 1961 and is now only 0·42%.'

(This text is provided by the New Abolitionists as the basis for letters to the press in order to help mould public opinion.)